The New Retirementality

The New Retirementality

PLANNING YOUR LIFE AND LIVING YOUR DREAMS . . . AT ANY AGE YOU WANT

FIFTH EDITION

Mitch Anthony

Published by John Wiley & Sons, Inc., Hoboken, New Jersey.

Published simultaneously in Canada.

For general information on our other products and services or for technical support, please contact our Customer Care Department within the United States at (800) 762-2974, outside the United States at (317) 572-3993, or fax (317) 572-4002.

Wiley publishes in a variety of print and electronic formats and by print-on-demand. Some material included with standard print versions of this book may not be included in e-books or in print-on-demand. If this book refers to media such as a CD or DVD that is not included in the version you purchased, you may download this material at http://booksupport.wiley.com. For more information about Wiley products, visit www.wiley.com.

Library of Congress Cataloging-in-Publication Data:

Names: Anthony, Mitch, author.

Title: The new retirementality : planning your life and living your dreams...at any age you want / Mitch Anthony.

Description: Fifth edition. | Hoboken, New Jersy : Wiley, [2020] | Includes index.

Identifiers: LCCN 2019033357 (print) | LCCN 2019033358 (ebook) | ISBN 9781119611486 (paperback) | ISBN 9781119611578 (ePDF) | ISBN 9781119611530 (ePub)

Subjects: LCSH: Retirement—United States. | Older people—United States—Finance, Personal.

Classification: LCC HQ1064.U5 A69 2020 (print) | LCC HQ1064.U5 (ebook) | DDC 306.3/80973—dc23

LC record available at https://lccn.loc.gov/2019033357

LC ebook record available at https://lccn.loc.gov/2019033358

Cover Design: Wiley
Cover Image: © Brostock/iStock.com

Printed in the United States of America

V10015702_112019

This book is dedicated to my mother,
Bettie Anthony Huntley,
who has never been afraid to
blaze her own trails and follow her instincts.
A generous portion of her spirit
guides my life as well.

Contents

Preface   **xi**

Acknowledgments   **xiii**

Chapter 1   A Short History of Retirement   1
               Crossing the Bridge   8

Chapter 2   Removing Artificial Finish Lines   9
               Dates of Extraction   11
               What Made Jack Dull?   13
               Motivated by Autonomy   14
               Illusions, Delusions, and Hype   16

Chapter 3   No Longer One and Done   19
               Stages of Grief?   20
               The Four Stages of LEAN   21
               The Balance Sheet   28
               Forced or Phased?   28
               Advocates Needed   30

Chapter 4   The New IRA: Individual Retirement
               Attitude   33
               Assume You Will Work Longer   36
               Assume You Will Live Longer   37
               Assume That There Will Be Improvisational
               Challenges   39

Chapter 5   Boredom Isn't on Anyone's Bucket List   43
Monotone Living   44
How You're Wired   45
When Frustration Replaces Fascination   45
Realistic Expectations   46
For Better or Worse but *Not* for Lunch   49
Losing Your Identity   49
The Rearview Mirror   50

Chapter 6   A New Mind-Set: Retire on Purpose   53
"I'm Done"   55
"I Have To"   55
"I'm Inspired"   56
Meaningful Pursuits: A Midlife Crisis Gone
Horribly Right   58
Enduring Attitudes   63

Chapter 7   Money Is Only Part of the Equation:
Investing Yourself, Then Your Money   67
A Very Long Trip   69
Where from Here?   71

Chapter 8   The Retirement That Works   79
Redefining Work   80
Longevity Works   83
Ready, Set, Engage   84
Retirement Planning That Works   86

Chapter 9   Extending Your Stay by Staying on
the Edge   89
Staying in Your Zone   90
Yes Sir, Kiddo   91
Ageism on the Radar   93
The Teaching Bridge   94
Advantages of Underemployment   95
EntreMature   96

Chapter 10 Super-Septs: How 70 Became the
New 50   101
Feeling as Fact   102
Your View of You   103
Turning the Corner   107
A New Season   108

Chapter 11 Redefining *You*: What's Your
Retirementality?   109
New Spin on Re-tiring   110

Chapter 12 Redefining Rich: Bridging the Gap
between Means and Meaning   121
The Seven Meaningful Intangibles   124
The Stewardship of Money   130

Chapter 13 Maslow Meets Retirement   133
More Than Just Money   134
Our Hierarchy of Financial Needs   136
Paying the Bills   140

Chapter 14 Advice from Retirementors   143
The Realities of Retirement   143
Retiremyths   146
Vacation: Balancing Work and Play   151
The Best (and Worst) Experiences   153
Allocation   154

Chapter 15 From Aging to S-Aging   157
A Sense of Mastery   158
The Vitamin Cs of Successful Aging   160
Challenge Your Body, Mind, and Spirit   166

Chapter 16 Don't Go It Alone   169
We Don't Always Know What We Don't Know   170
We Are Tempted to Follow the Crowd   171

Individual Investors Historically Underperform
the Indexes because They React Emotionally
to Market Events   172
It Is Time-Consuming and Stressful to
Manage Money on a Day-to-Day or
Week-to-Week Basis   172
Holding Your Ground   174
Finding a Wealth-Building Partner   175
A Personal Safety Net   177

Notes   **179**

About the Author   **187**

Index   **189**

Preface

The world continues to awaken to the realities of this strange institution we have created called *retirement*. Ideas that sounded novel when I first wrote them down 18 years ago now appear to be fairly common sentiment. My inspiration for this fifth edition has come from both the 60-plus rebels who have decided to live life on their own terms, as well as insights from those much younger.

For example, when Ryan was six years old, he visited with me in my library, where we discussed life, writing, and other macro themes that prevail upon the minds of precocious kindergartners. Ryan is quite possibly a writer-in-waiting. He is also the son of my wife's horse trainer. Shortly after our visit, his mother sent this note to me:

> One day I was explaining what "retirement" meant to my son Ryan. He looked at me in a very puzzled way after digesting the meaning of this strange concept and then said to me, "Mommy, when I get older I will never retire because I am going to love my job." After pondering the concept for a minute longer he continued, "And you will never retire either, will you, Mommy? Because you love your job, too, right?" I just laughed and reassured him that "No, I will probably never retire either because I truly do love my job." I smiled and thought how lucky he was at the young age of six to already have so much figured out. If only we could have more people entering our workforce with the focus not on that magical date of retirement, but rather on enjoying their journey through life and making the most of each day. Bless our sweet children for reminding us what is important in life . . .

Ryan instinctively understood, in viewing the idea through the innocent lens of the soul, that retirement—as it has been fashioned

and formed over the past 100 years—comes woefully short of helping human beings optimize their time on this planet. Our world
was sold the idea that this stage of life was best lived in consumption behind the walls of gated villages instead of contribution in the
world at large. Nothing could be further from the truth.

Money is part and parcel of the retirement discussion but is not
the primary component, despite the modern cultural inferences
of the term "retirement planning." What needs to be planned for
is much bigger than the accumulation and distribution of your
means. Having the means to retire is important. But what we also
must plan for—but often don't—is meaning. Age is irrelevant when
we discuss meaning at the individual level. Read and explore this
book with an open mind and an even wider heart and I am confident that you, too, will cross the bridge toward the most meaningful stage of life yet.

Acknowledgments

This book has an audience primarily because of the belief and encouragement provided by literary agent and publishing consultant Cynthia Zigmund, who has had her hand in all five editions of this book. Amazing, really.

Whatever degree of refinement the reader finds in this text is due to the ever watchful and always caring eye of my wife and first-line editor, Debbie.

I wish to acknowledge the many people who have written and told their stories to me of finding and maintaining purpose in their "second life." Many of these stories can be found within this text and they have all provided inspiration within me to keep the flame of this message burning.

M.A.

CHAPTER

A Short History of Retirement

When I want to understand what is happening today, I try to
decide what will happen tomorrow; I look back; a page of history is
worth a volume of logic.

—Oliver Wendell Holmes

The U.S. standard-gauge railroad track is four feet, eight and
one-half inches wide. Why such an odd measure? Because that was
the width in England and the United States when railroads were
built by British expatriates.

Where did the English get that measure? The first rail lines were
built by the same people who built the tramways that preceded railroads, and they built the trams with the same jigs and tools used for
building wagons. The wagons were built to the width of what is now
the standard-gauge railroad track so that their wheels would fit the
ruts of England's ancient roads.

The ruts had been made by the chariots brought to England by
the imperial Roman army. And the chariots were four feet, eight
and one-half inches wide to accommodate the rear ends of two
horses. You're not alone if you struggle with change.

Retirement as we know it today is a relic from a time and a
world that have long since passed. In the context of our modern
age, conventional ideas about retirement are not just inappropri-
ate—they are counterproductive. The concept of retirement was a

shortsighted political machination and social manipulation that is hopelessly out of touch with our times. Retirement is an unnatural phase in the modern life course. It is inserted between work and death and is irrelevant for those seeking to live a purposeful life. It is instructive for all of us to learn about the genesis of this life phase, which was invented by a past society for purposes that no longer apply to most of us.

Retirement, as we understand it today, did not exist in preindustrial America. In those days, older members of society weren't sent to the sidelines. They actually held a prominent position in their families and their society, respected for their insight, knowledge of skills and crafts, and lessons gained from experience. It was the Industrial Age that ushered in a profound redefinition of work and gave us the traditional notion of retirement. Mass production became the common mode of work, and workers began to be viewed as parts in the system, subject to wear and replaceable.

With the advent of industrialization came a population shift from the country to the cities. This brought about a significant lifestyle adjustment as people went from self-sufficiency to dependency. Work became a means to an end—an income to live on—as opposed to a way of life. In his book *The Sociology of Retirement* (John Wiley & Sons, 1976), Robert C. Atchley made an insightful comparison between a craftsman and a worker. A craftsman controls the process and the product, which makes his work both satisfying and integral to his or her identity. An industrial worker is responsible for one small part of the process. Consequently, the work offers little reward. Atchley also noted that the words "job" and "occupation" soon began to replace the terms *craft* and *vocation* in the American laborer's lexicon. Terms like *apprenticeship, avocation,* and *calling* also became passé as workers acclimated to punching the time clock and crossing days off the calendar in anticipation of the day they could retire.

We can trace a cycle of degradation of the American work ethic to this point in history, which comes as no surprise: one would naturally expect people to become lethargic about work that offers no emotional reward.

As other nations were embracing industrialization, the world became a competitive commercial environment. America was intent on proving itself to be a world leader, and progress was the mantra of the industrialists. As a result, these industrialists began looking for ways to sweep away anything that stood in the path of that progress. For some of them a major obstacle to progress was anyone considered "mature" in age. Because of advances in safety and health care, people were living longer, and the workforce was getting older. Mature workers were beginning to be viewed as a threat to progress. It was assumed that older people would not acclimate easily to changing procedures, and changes were needed for industry to become an efficient, well-oiled machine. The seeds of ageism were beginning to be sown. Those seeds of prejudice were watered well over a century ago by a widely reported speech by Dr. William Osler, one of the nation's most prominent physicians, given in 1905 at Johns Hopkins University. Osler's thesis was that any man over 40 years old was virtually useless to society.

"Take the sum of human achievement in action, in science, in art, in literature," Osler said. "Subtract the work of men above 40, and while we would miss great treasures, even priceless treasures, we would practically be where we are today." In short, Osler was postulating that any person over 40 was dispensable to the cause of progress. Osler went on to say that people over 60 were "entirely useless" and a drain on society because of their inelastic minds. Osler's articulation helped to embolden a growing intellectual trend and opportunistically served to answer the growing societal problem of unemployment. It seemed obvious, these intellectuals asserted, to replace the old with the new. All that was left was to come up with a way to get rid of the old. Mandatory retirement was one answer.[1]

Another emerging force in this drama was the labor union that was struggling to survive and fighting for the right to strike. Labor unions quickly embraced the idea of retirement because forcing out the older workers gave them the opportunity to deliver the jobs and job security they were promising their membership. Business leaders, labor leaders, and social engineers were all singing the retirement chorus. Older workers didn't have a chance—and soon wouldn't have a choice.

There was, however, one massive obstacle standing in the way of this strategy. What would these new retirees live on? In the late nineteenth century, Chancellor Otto von Bismarck had come up with a disability insurance program in the German Empire for all disabled workers aged 70 years and older. This was instituted by von Bismarck in part to undermine demands for democracy and to reaffirm workers' commitment to the government. Around that same time, American Express created the first private pension in America in 1875.[2] In 1900 the Pattern Makers League of North America became the first union to offer pensions to its members. Up until that time, pensions were typically available only to veterans and civil servants such as policemen and firefighters, and, in some states, teachers.

It was not until 1910 that the pension movement gained steam. That year, William Howard Taft's administration started promoting pensions as a major piece of its platform on industrial efficiency. From 1910 to 1920, more than 200 new pension plans were formed. A change in the corporate tax law that made pension plans more tax advantageous resulted in the doubling of new plans in 1920. Overall, the penetration rate for pensions was quite slow, with only 15% of American workers covered by a plan by 1932. The watershed moment came in 1933, in the deepest, darkest depths of the Great Depression. Social conditions had reached an explosive point because of the 25% unemployment rate. Franklin D. Roosevelt and the New Dealers were in a precarious and potentially disastrous situation, with masses of angry young men demonstrating in the streets. Roosevelt had already seen where these situations could lead by the examples set in Germany and Italy. It was exactly these conditions that gave rise to both Hitler and Mussolini. The New Dealers' plan to get young people working again was to offer a public pension so the older men would retire.

Combine this reality with the fact that a movement was afoot with the elderly to demand pensions for those over 60. People wanted the federal government to get involved. At that time, 28 states had pension programs—which made little difference in the lives of the recipients because the programs were sparsely funded as a result of the Great Depression. Many corporate pensions were defaulting as well. As a result, 50% of the elderly were living in poverty.

The New Dealers needed to test their plan before implementing it on a national scale. Would the older workers like the idea? Senator Robert F. Wagner introduced a bill in 1934 establishing a pension for retiring railroad workers. Wagner compelled 50,000 workers to consider retiring immediately. The bill passed. Wagner played a major role in 1935 in persuading FDR to introduce the Older Workers Pension Act, later called the Social Security Act—the statute that would forever change our views of work and retirement. However, Roosevelt had to settle two major issues that would echo through the generations. How would Social Security be paid for, and at what age would workers become eligible? This Social Security program would not work if it failed to provide instant benefits for those who were currently at the retirement age. Rather than taxing these people for their own retirement, elected officials came up with the idea of taxing those who were still working on behalf of retirees. Tax the younger generation to pay for the retiring generation. When the Social Security Act was implemented, the number of beneficiaries was small enough that no one would have to pay much for the plan.

Now the biggest question had to be answered: At what age can one receive Social Security? Precedents existed at the time in Germany, Great Britain, and France, with ages pegged to 60, 65, and 70. Citing a biblical reference to "threescore and ten years," Bismarck's original retirement marker was set at 70, allowing the workers enough time to pick out a gravestone should they be lucky enough to live much longer. Eighteen years later, Germany lowered the age to 65 because very few people lived to 70 to collect the benefits; the average life expectancy at that time was only 46 years!

The retirement plans designed by Bismarck and others had obviously not been intended to give a worker any time for enjoyment—not with a life expectancy of 46 and a retirement age of 65. It helps to move to our modern age to understand Bismarck's original intent. The age of retirement was 19 years beyond the average life expectancy. In those days a person who was 65 was indeed old—much older than today's 65-year-old.

When FDR and the New Dealers settled on the age of 65 in 1935, the average life expectancy in America was 63 years. Bear in mind, however, that life expectancy statistics can be misleading because factors such as infant mortality are calculated into them. According to the Social Security Administration, the average number of years lived in retirement today hasn't changed much since 1935, increasing only about five years during that period.[3]

But it is important to remember that the population of those over 65 has increased dramatically in our time. According to the Population Reference Bureau, Americans 65 and older are projected to more than double from 46 million (as of 2015) to over 98 million by 2060.[4]

The obvious conclusion one could make is that retirement was never intended to remove people with strong productivity potential out of the workplace. Our view is skewed on this issue, however, as a result of the difference in the constitution of a 65-year-old today and that of a 65-year-old in 1935. Because the retirement markers were set later than the average life expectancy, many people didn't live long enough to collect Social Security benefits. FDR eventually moved to have the age of retirement set to age 62.

The benefits that a retiree did receive were just enough to support a meager lifestyle, providing bare sustenance. It was this generation of retirees that evoked the images of widows wearing long winter coats while sitting in cold, decrepit one-room apartments and eating cat food to survive. It would take another 20 years before the social net and workplace invention known as retirement would become a part of the American way of life.

The retirement lifestyle got a major boost during World War II when workers' wages were frozen. Because wages were non-negotiable, union leaders began bargaining for pensions where they didn't exist and for bigger employer contributions where they did exist. These contributions were tax deductible, and future pension obligations weren't reflected in a company's balance sheet. World War II conditions caused pension coverage to flourish across most industries. The timing could not have been better for the Social Security system, which was being roundly criticized for allowing retirees to live in poverty. Opportunistic politicians in the following decades began to push for broadened coverage to include husbands of working women, farmers, the self-employed, members of the armed forces, and so on. Coverage itself was expanded to include health and disability insurance, welfare for the disabled, and, as an answer to the senior poverty issue, annual cost-of-living adjustments to keep up with inflation.

With all these changes, retirement began to shed its destitute and forsaken image. Combining Social Security payments with pension checks allowed people to live a respectable, if modest, retirement—but it still typically lasted only a year or two at best. It was during this period of retirement's image transition that financial services companies stepped up their efforts. They began to market retirement as an individual's rightful reward for his or her years of labor and loyal service. People began buying more retirement investment products and looked forward to an era of reward that would be timed on their new gold watch.

William Graebner, in his *History of Retirement* (Yale University Press, 1980), shares an interesting anecdote regarding a shift in the financial services industry's marketing of retirement. The story is told that in 1952, H. G. Kenagy of Mutual Life Insurance advised business leaders on the National Industrial Conference Board about the best way to sell retirement to their employees. The approach he suggested was distributing stories by these business leaders via company newsletters and the like about happily retired people fishing or playing golf and sipping martinis. Sell the blissful retirement life and don't forget to mention how to get to nirvana by investing in both the company plan and other financial vehicles. This was not a difficult story to sell to a workforce that now had jobs instead of vocations. As one 82-year-old non-retiree put it, "They that lack a vocation are always longing for a vacation." Retirement had now become the permanent vacation—without the kids!

Almost 70 years later, this retirement pitch from 1952 has hardly changed. Although some firms in the retirement products industry are catching on to the philosophical shift regarding what people really want out of their longer lives, many companies in the industry lag woefully behind, with antiquated images of fishing ponds, beaches, and golf courses.

People began to retire in unprecedented numbers because (1) they felt they had to or were forced by retirement age policy to do so; and (2) the unexpected appreciation in home prices made comfortable retirement a real possibility. The implied message to workers: "You don't have a choice. Once you hit 62 (or 65) you're out the door." No employers were begging them to stay around for a while or willing to just cut back their hours. It was universally accepted that you were no longer welcome in the working world at retirement age.

Crossing the Bridge

We have, in years past, had our brains pummeled with warnings that we should save more if we hope to leap off the economic cliff known as "retirement" at age 62. Many of us had been convinced that we wanted to jump off that cliff earlier—if possible, much earlier. But, today, we understand that the new retirement resembles a bell curve rather than a cliff. Rather than jumping off a vocational cliff, we will gradually slow down.

The metaphor that I believe is more fitting for our age is that of a bridge between full-time work and full-time retirement. The length of the bridge varies from person to person, and the bridge can appear for any length of time and can be entered and exited multiple times in the post-60 years. And there are some of us who want to do the work we do as long as we possibly can—meaning as long as we are healthy and competent, we will be on that bridge.

Back in 2009 a new realization around retirement dawned as the result of the confluence of an asset-eroding economy and a cultural epiphany around retirement. The great recession convinced millions that a longer work life would be necessary, and many of those who had retired were returning to at least part-time work because they found something missing in the traditional vision of retirement.

The reality we are left with is that most of us will work longer than previously expected but not necessarily for reasons we assumed. Yes, economic incentives will play a role as many of us seek to replenish retirement funds or extend benefits, but the incentives don't begin and end with your checkbook—they are much more holistic than previously understood. Many of us are choosing to work longer for our own well-being, for the well-being of a relationship, and for the well-being of society.

CHAPTER

Removing Artificial Finish Lines

While one finds company in himself and his pursuits, he cannot feel old, no matter what his years may be.

—Amos Alcott

Mapmakers in medieval times faced a problem. They were given the job of charting the continent but were not exactly well-traveled themselves. So when they came to a border they had not crossed, they drew fire-breathing dragons facing their own country's boundaries. These maps, when viewed by the common masses, caused people to believe that if they crossed the border, they would be consumed by these infernal beasts. Needless to say, this limited travel and adventure. Many people, when challenged to try new things, to go to new places, or to try doing things in a different way, simply refuse. When asked, "Why?" they simply respond, "I'm too old"—it's as though they've been looking at aging maps with dragons.

Lydia Bronte wrote *The Longevity Factor* over 25 years ago (HarperCollins, 1993), but her conclusions sound prophetic and eerily familiar, considering what we are witnessing even more frequently today. In her observations of a long careers study, she wrote:

> What emerges from their life stories is a view of the long life-time different from what we might expect: an affirmation of the increasing richness of experience over time, of a deeper

sense of identity, of a greater self-confidence and creative potential that can grow rather than diminish with maturity. It is obvious that seen through the eyes of the study participants, chronological age markers (like 65), which have held so much power in the past, are really culturally created—a norm that was accurate only for a particular place and time.

Why is it that when we talk of the maturity of money, we think of it as a positive form of growth; but when we talk about the maturity of people, we think of it as a time of depreciation? Within a decade or so, we will see multitudinous examples of a great harvest of accomplishment and contribution coming after the ages of 65, 75, and even 85. There are thousands of examples out there right now—we just need to take notice. We can all try new ventures: we can all stretch our limitations, our abilities, our contributions, our reach, and our grasp. Each of us has the ability to test our endurance a bit further. Without taking risks, we settle into a quicksand called *complacency*.

The only thing that has ever made me feel old is those few times where I allow myself to be predictable. Routine is death.
—Carlos Santana

How old is old? What exactly do we mean when we say someone is old? Are we referring to the person's years on the planet or their state of being? Or both? By old, do we mean that a person is in a state of decline? Is there a predictable age when this decline commences for all people? Is "old" a manmade border? And do the dragons of decline exist mostly in our mind? Henry Ford said that when a person stops learning, he is old, whether that person is 29 or 65. As you will discover throughout this book, there isn't much we can do about aging, but there is an awful lot we can do about growing old. We hold "old" at bay by focusing on successful aging.

Satchel Paige was arguably the best pitcher to ever play professional baseball. It is estimated that he won over 800 games in his unparalleled career. Because of racial boundaries, he didn't get the opportunity to display his talents outside the Negro leagues until the color barrier was broken by Jackie Robinson.

When Paige did get his chance to pitch in the major leagues, he was elected the American League Rookie of the Year at the age of 43! Think about that. There is a very short list of men who have possessed the endurance to pitch at age 43. Paige was the Rookie of the Year at that age! He pitched in the majors until he was in his early 50s and continued to pitch professionally until he was 63 years old. Paige understood a few things about longevity.

Because of preconceptions about age and ability, Paige always tried to keep his age a mystery. Whenever he was queried about his age, he would provide a memorable quip like, "How old would you be if you didn't know how old you were?" or "I never look back on Father Time—he might be gaining on me."

We have many high-profile examples of achievers in our culture who are not looking back on Father Time, including Warren Buffett, still a leader in investment acumen in his upper 80s.

You probably have some great examples of "ageless wonders" in your own community. Study their example, their lifestyle, and, most important, their attitude. When I question these ageless phenoms, they always mention attitude as a key to thriving, regardless of age. Just as the ages of 62 and 65 are artificial finish lines for retirement, so also are any other ages that people cite when saying "he (or she) is too old for that." People are actively skiing in their 80s, racing in their 90s, walking and swimming in their 100s. Some people are working into their 11th decade. Examples of people crashing through age barriers and jumping over physical limitation hurdles are ubiquitous. A while back, I received a video from a family that had four generations perform a synchronized water-skiing exhibition in North Carolina: their ages were 5, 40, 62, and 92!

Dates of Extraction

Most people say when you get old you have to give things up, but I think we get old because we give things up.

—Theodore Green
(Senator Green was 98 when he retired in 1966.)

Only you have the right to announce a verdict on your date of extraction. The employment of your skills, competencies, and ideas should be for as long as you desire. None of us comes into this world with "use by" dates stamped on our backs. As long as we enjoy utilizing our competencies and truly love what we do, we should never quit the race. We may slow our pace or change the event we run in, but we should never stop participating.

Do you really want to quit working? Sadly, because so many people are working in jobs, industries, and offices they hate, they have convinced themselves that the answer is to stop working (a.k.a., retirement). But the fact remains that most of us wouldn't be obsessed with the idea of quitting if we were doing what we wanted to do in the first place.

Maybe the real truth is that you want to quit what you are currently doing to be able to do something else; you need or want a change but are convinced that you need a mountain of money to make the switch. You decide to postpone your dreams, assuming that when you finally do have the money, you will still have the desire and drive necessary to follow your dreams. People in these circumstances— and there are many—need to contemplate the psychologically sobering fact that as they drive themselves in a career they dislike (or worse, despise), they are driving on tires with a slow leak. The ride gets rougher and tougher until they find their aspirations in the ditch and little energy left to begin a new journey. This is what happens when you chase an artificial finish line.

Why have so many of us given our lives to work we don't enjoy? The reason is simply that we need the money. Why do we need the money? So we can have enough to retire at age 62 and finally do what we want. Great! You've just sacrificed 40 prime productive years in order to have a speculative, free rein for the autumn and/or winter years.

Doing work we despise or being in circumstances we deplore depletes our spirit. The reason many of us find ourselves in such scenarios is that we have been sold on an idea about retirement that is flawed to the core: the idea that we should do what we do not enjoy to accumulate the money we need to someday do what we want. This hope of doing what we really want to do is why the concept of traditional retirement is alluring to so many. Too many of us are not on the track we want to run on. We see getting to the age of 62 with enough money as the only way to get there. When you're on the wrong track, any finish line will do.

If the coming generation of 60-plus-year-old citizens has anything to say about it, those perceptions will be turned entirely on their head. Those who have to work will not be the losers, because they are still in the game—they will find that work keeps them vital, involved, and healthier. Those who will be able to drop out entirely will choose not to because they don't want to enter a slow track of intellectual atrophy, boredom, and monotonous leisure.

What Made Jack Dull?

Is accelerating your pace into boredom—"every day's a Saturday" all-play agenda—really such a good idea? Unlike the nursery rhyme we learned as children, it's really "all play and no work" that makes Jack a dull boy. The illusion has been that of sipping tropical drinks on a Caribbean beach and setting tee times for the rest of your life. "All this is yours" once you retire, and the earlier you retire, the better. Possibly you've met some people who swallowed this illusion and are living with the hangover of boredom and purposelessness in their lives.

I have met many such people, and the look in their eyes inspired me to write this book. Many who bought the story of retiring from the race find themselves bored with not being in the race. Many have found that this boredom led to self-destructive patterns of behavior. Many have accelerated their aging process as the chains of disenfranchised habits have grown heavier and weighed on their health. It all adds up to one inescapable conclusion: retirement is an unnatural condition. Even if you can afford to retire, the worst thing you can do is to withdraw completely from the track of relevance.

Although you may not have heard much about it, those who do get to the magic age of 62 and drop out of the race are not always altogether happy with their decision. Many have told me that they took retirement because they felt as though they had to. Disillusionment rates are high for ambivalent retirees. According to a survey conducted by AARP and the Society for Human Resource

Management, 20% of U.S. companies have programs in place to phase employees into retirement to avoid just such disillusionment. There is a good reason these retirees are not happy—retirement is an unnatural idea. The concept runs contrary to the preservation of the human spirit. We will explore this idea in depth throughout this book.

If you're eligible for Social Security, tired of the grind, and ready to cross the finish line, that's a different story. Go for it. Just don't be surprised if you find yourself searching for productive engagements soon thereafter. Choose your own finish line—don't let someone else choose it for you.

Motivated by Autonomy

Most people don't really want retirement in the form we've observed during the past few generations. What we want is freedom to pursue our own goals and interests. We want autonomy to call our own shots. We want to do what we want, when we want, and where we want. We want change if our employment has become a dispiriting rut. We have been told that the right amount of money alone can buy that emancipation. And, if we believed that message, we may have settled into that rut and postdated our satisfaction for a time in the distant future. Our artificial finish line beckoned to us.

And that is why we are so vulnerable to the messages that tell us we need $2 to $3 million to set ourselves free. But this simply is not true. I will not argue that having money gives you options—it does. If you have enough, you can usually do things the way you want. But financial abundance is not the exclusive seed bed for autonomy. Willfulness with resourcefulness is the more potent soil for finding a life that satisfies.

This book tells stories of people who are living the life they want—today—and not all have a million dollars in assets or investments. Because of outdated ideas around retirement, we have put the money cart ahead of the "life" horse. We say we are saving money so that we can someday have a life, but in the process we delay having a life so that we can scrounge up enough money. Too many of us wait far too long to realize that the life we are living right now is not a dress rehearsal.

With some financial creativity and a new mindset regarding retirement, you can both find and fund the life you really want—if not now, it is entirely possible within the next five years. Achieving emancipation in your working life will involve negotiating your lifestyle and fiscal habits and finding a way to put first things first. First, decide the path you must take to do the work you love, and, second, put together a plan to pay for that privilege. All of us must adopt a much more resourceful approach if we hope to make the transition into a life of doing what we love. It won't necessarily be easy, but it will be worth it.

We are still in the early stages of a New Retirementality—a modern perspective of what retirement really means. People are still haunted by the old rules and media hype that bemoan their lack of preparedness to reach the artificial goal line. We just can't seem to get away from the news stories, retirement studies, and advertisements that beat this sorry old retirement message to death.

There is no doubt that as a society, we could exercise more discipline in our savings habits. Indeed, it wouldn't really harm us in the present to put more assets away toward our future. However, putting money away toward your future and putting money away toward your extraction from the work engagement are two different matters.

This point became especially clear to me recently when a friend asked me if I had plans to retire early. I think the only reason he asked was because he knew I was nearing 60 years of age. I thought about it for a moment, and then it dawned on me—I like what I do! I write, speak, and consult with companies on how to build more meaningful relationships. Why would I quit doing that? If I did quit, I think I would begin to feel aimless and lost. This realization, which came to me many years ago, was important because it helped me to realize that I no longer had to be concerned with having any specific amount of money at any specific age. There will always be something for me to do, and I will always enjoy doing it. You don't make plans to retire from your passion in life.

Does this idea cause me to spend away my future and disregard the value of my investment savings? To the contrary! Because I value freedom so much, I exercise more than necessary financial discipline to maintain that freedom. The idea of autonomy compels me, motivating me to exercise financial discipline in what I spend and what I save. I love my life, and I'm not going to put it at risk because I didn't have the prudence to put away a ransom toward my own freedom.

I know that I am just one foolish purchase or investment away from reattaching the chains of miserable employment to my life. There is wisdom in balance. The fact that I love what I do does not negate the need to plan for financial freedom. Life can present us with vicissitudes that can radically alter our course: disability, a death in the family, divorce, and so on. We must plan ahead financially because we change our minds over time. What invigorates me today may bore me a decade from today. Investment savings are necessary to purchase the freedom to change course when we want. I find this idea much more compelling than saving toward a date where I will magically find myself, my dreams, and the freedom to do what I've waited 30-plus years to do. Yet I find it troubling, because of the constant media barrage and the financial services–induced discouragement, how many people are concerned about their inability to "retire" at 62 or 65. Can we have a break from this manmade definition of success and take a closer look at reality?

Strangely enough, millions are in a mad rush to get to the sidelines. Many of us, however, have already seen enough of our parents' and forerunners' retirement scenarios to know that this is not the life for us. We have figured out that our lives will be full of challenge, relevance, stimulation, and adventure. We may slow down, but we are not leaving the track for the concession stand.

The fortunate people who have the money are better able to understand what the money is all about—freedom to do what they want when they want. What is the point of using that kind of freedom to do nothing but play golf? It's hard to convince someone who doesn't have the money that it really is not about the money. It's about doing what you love, doing what you want. It's about balancing vocation and vacation. It's about balancing enrichment and relationships.

Illusions, Delusions, and Hype

Yet the drumbeat of "you won't have enough to retire" pounds on like a Sousa march without regard to the cultural realizations we are experiencing around the retirement experience of our parents and forerunners into the gated community existence. We will be hearing these messages for the foreseeable future until some marketing executives wake up and realize that making people feel worse about what they don't have isn't a great ploy for motivating the masses.

According to *The 2018 Northwestern Mutual Planning & Progress Study*, 1 in 3 Americans have less than $5,000 saved for retirement.[1] For the millions of Americans who don't own a fat nest egg, these messages stir feelings of hopelessness because they are convinced that they will arrive at the age 62 economic leap with no safety net or precious metals parachute based on their current income and level of savings. They know they will never be able to amass the small fortune that "retirement experts" tell them they must hoard to have anything but a beggar's sunset in their life. The modern retirement portrait, as painted by the financial services industry, is truly a double-headed dragon, because the vision that has been promoted for the past 50 years is not only an illusion but is also unrealistic.

When you ask many retirees how they're doing, they often reply, "I'm keeping busy." This is an acknowledgment of the activity void that retirement has brought. Most humans are truly happy when they are busy doing what they love. If they are not busy doing what they love, they are most likely not very happy.

The image of retirement that we have been sold has simply been untrue. According an Employee Benefits Research Institute study, less than 48.6% of retirees reported being "highly satisfied" (versus 60.5% previously) while almost 10.5% reported being "not at all satisfied" (versus 7.9% previously).[2] The reason the adjustment to retirement is difficult to so many is simple: retirement as it has been defined for us was never meant to be.

Which brings us to the dragon's other head: many of us cannot afford to retire in the manner that has been promoted by the retirement savings industry. It is simply unrealistic for us to find a way to put away enough money every month to have millions waiting to serve us at age 62, or at any other age for that matter.

But why should a significant percentage of us, who are doing our best with what we have, walk around feeling discouraged about today because we cannot reach a tomorrow that somebody else has defined for us? We have been given the various ominous headlines for our future: "Social Security will not exist, you don't have sufficient savings, and inflation will eat up what little you do have." According to the 2017/2018 Global Benefits Attitudes Survey, more than one-third of all U.S. workers expect to retire at 70 or higher.[3] The most profound problem I see with pervasive and frequently reported scare tactics is that these arguments are founded on a fabricated and now crumbling philosophical foundation—that is, we should retire at age 62 or 65. Many of us will not completely retire at 65, and many will not retire at all. And one of the chief drivers of this trend will not be that we simply cannot afford to retire—it will be because we are not interested in artificial finish lines.

No Longer One and Done

When I first started working many years ago, I would hear of retirees who had decided to pull the string on their "golden parachute" and head to the sidelines. To me, this was an interesting metaphor that implied not only a safe landing but a necessary leap in order to achieve that safe landing.

I'm guessing the analogy had something to do with Richard Bolles's bestselling book, *What Color Is Your Parachute?* first published in 1970 and updated every year beginning in 1975. Originally self-published by Bolles, it has become the job hunters' and career changers' bible through the years. The specific parachute reference I'm alluding to was code for a lucrative financial retirement package that led someone to pull the cord and make the leap into a new lifestyle.

When I first heard comments about gold or platinum parachutes, our corporate cultures were just beginning the shift from paternalistic pensions to self-directed retirement accounts—the latter the result of actuaries determining that pension plans were unsustainable. This chapter is not about the financial shift in the concept of retirement but the *characterization of the shift*, from the former leap to a less dramatic, more thoughtful segue I describe as the L.E.A.N. into retirement. This four-stage approach lets us "lean into" retirement instead of leaping headfirst and hoping we get it right:

Looking Ahead
Embarking
After the Honeymoon
Negotiating Balances

We've already known that diving from full-time work to full-time leisure is a drastic leap and not healthy. People have organically begun to make the change in stages—mini-journeys, if you will—to make the lifestyle redefinition feel more natural than a sudden switch from cubicle at HQ to a captain's chair in the RV.

Stages of Grief?

The need for recharacterizing the retirement transition became clear to me when I received a call from a journalist doing a story on the correlation of the retirement transition and the stages of grief:

Denial, Anger, Bargaining, Depression, and Acceptance

Wow.

The reason the journalist was doing the story was obvious—many people's retirement transitions have led them through these stages. It need not be so. The reason so many people have had such experiences is because of the way they are encouraged to make the change: suddenly and all at once. Set a target date, get your finances in order, wait for the day, and LEAP! Good luck, by the way.

Some retirees ease smoothly into retirement by spending more time with family, friends, or hobbies they find intriguing. But researchers have found that others experience anxiety, as well as feelings of loss and depression. According to Robert Delamontagne, PhD, "People can go through hell when they retire and they will never say a word about it, often because they are embarrassed." Delamontagne surmises the reason these people are embarrassed is because the supposed cultural norm for retirement is that you're now living the good life—if, by chance, you're not, then there might be something wrong with you.[1]

Or maybe there's something wrong with the system (and the sudden pace) of retirement that has been thrust upon us.

Retirement has long been depicted as a one-and-done proposition: you forecast or calculate an age where it might be most advantageous for you to retire, make the leap into the unknown, and learn to adjust along the way. Almost a decade ago, the Rand Un-Retirement study began telling a different story when it revealed that it takes most people three to four attempts at retirement to get to a place they're comfortable with.[2] I suspect that the chief reason for these multiple attempts is the errant characterization of the retirement transition.

(Reminder: I'm coming from a vantage point that retirement is still an unnatural act—and adjustment difficulties should be assumed when we force ourselves into a life-stage designed for us by outside forces.)

I think the reason that research showed people making the transition in three or four attempts is due to the organic path that is taken when retirees begin to change their minds and hearts to get comfortable with the downshift. With that organic leaning in mind, I'd like to propose that we begin talking about and taking the retirement shift in a staged approach.

The Four Stages of LEAN

Stage One: Looking Ahead

This stage could be 5 to 10 years ahead of the transition, or it could be 30 or more years ahead. I had my own "Looking Ahead" moment when I was 38 years old. I specifically remember the moment. In those days, because my work was tied to students and teachers, I essentially had the summers off. Being a golfer, I played every day I could during those summers.

One day while golfing with my wife, I had an eye-opening and sudden epiphany, and said to her, "When all I do is golf, I feel like I'm wasting all my creative and competitive energies on something, that in the end, pays few dividends. I don't think I could ever fully retire and have to depend on a hobby for my internal satisfaction."

This epiphany was a great gift at a young age. I realized that my work schedule (having the summer months off) had given me the opportunity to rehearse a retirement lifestyle and get a realistic internal assessment. I also realized this isn't possible for everyone, but if there is a way or means to have a practice run for yourself, I highly recommend it.

In the past decade, T. Rowe Price, a major retirement plan provider, started advocating the "practice retirement" idea and told investors that the idea had financial advantages as well as lifestyle rewards. The new paradigm looked something like this: keep working in your 60s but also start spending some of your current income, enjoying what could be the best decade of your life. Though you're spending some income on the fun stuff, you're still allowing both your retirement savings and your Social Security to grow toward receiving maximum benefit from both at age 70.[3]

With this approach you're test-driving some of the things you think you want to do and simultaneously reducing the number of years you'll need to fund in retirement (possibly from 35 to 25). The test driving of retirement would be an especially good idea for those who fantasize about an expensive RV in their future. Why not take a practice run before committing all your material and emotional resources to that journey?

Nathan Faith, a young financial advisor, had his epiphany (while reading an earlier version of this book). I was speaking to a group of his firm's clients when Nathan approached me and said,

> I know most of the people in this room are either within 10 years of retiring or already retired, but I want you to know this book changed me and my wife's lives when we read it in our early thirties. I had just started my career in financial services. Several clients had asked for a book to read as they considered their own transition towards retirement. My boss and mentor recommended your book to each of them. I decided to read it myself, hoping to be able to speak conceptually with clients. I did not expect the lessons to impact my wife and my life directly. After reading the first few chapters one night, I turned to my wife and explained that this was the first finance-related book that she should read and would enjoy. We were just starting out, living in a cramped apartment, experiencing life one day at a time. The epiphany we had was that too many of the people we knew were either delaying happiness too long or not at all. Most everyone we knew, young or less young, were letting fear or greed dictate how they lived their lives. We did not want the pursuit of money to interfere with our pursuit of happiness. Left to my own devices, I would have saved us into poverty during our platinum years and been left to wonder what to do with it during our golden years. My wife would have been more

on the other end of the spectrum. Because of your book, we had real conversations about moderation, compromise, and what we really wanted in our lives.

We set our priorities before they could be set for us, striving for a balance between our current and future selves. We chose savings goals that were a stretch to begin with but became less demanding as our incomes rose. We eventually chose to purchase a home that was comfortable instead of luxurious. Vehicles that were practical instead of showy. It was not all about sacrificing early: we chose to travel and take a warm vacation every year (but to resorts a quarter mile down the beach from Sandals).

Those early conversions and subsequent decisions have afforded us enviable flexibility that we did not ever anticipate. For instance, we always intended to start a family, but we did not anticipate how expensive daycare is. Unlike our friends and peers, instead of working harder to pay the bills, or cutting back on other priorities, we could afford to do the opposite. We chose to have the proverbial cake and eat it too. When our daughter was born two years ago, it was important for my wife to spend more time at home. We chose to reduce her commitment to work from five days a week to four. I too have cut back by choosing to do more of what I enjoy at work, and less of what I do not, to free up time for our family. These choices have reduced our income, yet did little to impact the cost of daycare. However, neither of us expects that we will ever regret the additional time with our children.

We are exceedingly happy and are confident about our present and our future. The New Retirementality provided the perspective we needed in order to have the genuine discussions about what we wanted.

The Faith family gave me faith that you can start planning your lives and living your dreams much earlier than most people think.

In looking ahead, I think a core exercise is a philosophical exam to determine if the concept of retirement is a good fit given your career path, enthusiasm about work, level of autonomy, and so on. Why spend the middle of your life aiming at an artificial finish line that you have no real interest in crossing? Also, if you know you can only do what you do for so much longer, why not begin making changes and taking steps earlier in life that will make that transition more viable? Don't wait until you're stuck both economically and professionally.

Rate your retirement concepts from 1 to 5, with 5 being the best fit for you.

Retirementality Philosophical Exam

I consider my work a mission in life.	1 2 3 4 5
I'm deeply energized by the work I do.	1 2 3 4 5
Being 60+ will not diminish my ability to deliver.	1 2 3 4 5
I'm in control of my career choices.	1 2 3 4 5
I have the say on how long I can work.	1 2 3 4 5
I get bored without challenges in front of me.	1 2 3 4 5
I'm not waiting until late in life to do "bucket list" items.	1 2 3 4 5
TOTAL	
28–35	You're a candidate for driving on. Don't plan on retiring. Save your money to ensure your autonomy and freedom to do what you want.
21–27	You're a candidate for switching lanes. Think about finding some other track at some point in your life that allows you the freedom to do what you want at the pace you choose.
7–21	You might be a good candidate for taking the exit ramp when you're financially able.

Stage Two: Embarking

This stage covers the period from six months before through six months after. It is the stage where you should conduct an examination of both time and money and make sure there is a proper correlation between those two resources. You'll want to sit down and do a retirement income projection and cash-flow analysis to determine the lifestyle you can afford. Many people fail to take this step and quickly learn that they're spending ahead of their resources and putting themselves at risk further down the retirement road.

I've also witnessed a strange psychological phenomenon with recent retirees that I call the "Captain Coupon" syndrome— an obsession with knowing how to save a buck on everything and everywhere. The reason for this sort of cost-saving reasoning is that retirees are suddenly hit with the impact of cashing their last paycheck and realizing that they have entered the economic twilight zone where their expenses will rise but their income won't. As time passes, this gap broadens and the mental space between income and expenses gets quickly filled with anxiety. This might explain the number of retirees staring at the stock ticker on CNBC and downing shots of Pepto-*Abysmal.*

If your income won't support your plans, then your plans will have to change in one of two ways: spend less or work longer. There aren't really any other options.

Early in this stage, I recommend that prospective retirees go through three preparative exercises:

1. A visioning exercise to help predict how you will occupy yourself for 168 hours a week when 40 to 50 of those hours are suddenly freed up. See the *Visioning* exercise in Chapter 7 and *My Ideal Week in Retirement* exercise in Chapter 11.
2. A reflective exercise on the value and benefits of work from a lifestyle and economic perspective. See the *Retirement Worksheet* in Chapter 7.
3. A retirement-persona profile in order to preempt a "couple's conundrum" in the first few months of retirement. See the *My Retirementality Profile* in Chapter 11.

These exercises will help immensely in avoiding a crash landing or suffering from retirement whiplash by surveying how you will utilize your time so you don't start feeling aimless or bored. The exercises will help you recognize the aspects of work you may find yourself missing so you can think about how to fill those potential voids. Finally, the exercises will help you to navigate the sometimes difficult transition with your significant other in unity and understanding.

Stage Three: After the Honeymoon

According to a study by Elizabeth Mokyr Horner, PhD, for the *Journal of Happiness Studies*, retirees experience a "sugar rush" of well-being and life satisfaction directly after retirement that is followed by a sharp decline in happiness a few years later. The subjects in the study were from 16 countries in western Europe and the United States. The rush-crash pattern showed up irrespective of the age at which the person retired.[4]

Dr. Horner states, "People are going to spend more time retired, even if we push the retirement age back. We need to figure out a way to maximize people's happiness." Experts believe that one answer might be to encourage more altruism in this stage (as opposed to the increased consumerism which has been encouraged for years as the retirement ideal). In a 2018 study in the *Journal of Aging and Health* led by Eva Kahans, PhD,[5] researchers discovered that people living in retirement communities reported higher levels of satisfaction and lower levels of depression if they were engaged in moderate levels of volunteer work than those who weren't.

But putting too much stock in volunteering activities can backfire as well. We have a more in-depth discussion on this topic in Chapter 14 where we discuss a study of 500 retirees that includes insights on the ups and downs of volunteering.

After 6 to 12 months of retirement living, most people have experienced a few reality checks, and ask themselves one or more of the following questions:

Am I experiencing loss of esteem issues since retiring?
Am I sleeping later?
Am I watching more television?
Am I getting less satisfaction from my hobbies?

Have I been less social?
Do I feel aimless at times?
Am I drinking more?
Do I feel less healthy than I did before retiring?
Have I been experiencing feelings of depression?
Am I being less communicative?
Am I sensing more tension in my marriage?

If you find yourself answering "yes" to three or more of these questions after the honeymoon phase of retirement—anywhere from 6 months to 1.5 years, depending on the individual—then it's time for you to enter stage four.

Stage Four: Negotiating Balances

When the initial sugar buzz of retirement wears off and the reality of filling your time with both enjoyable and meaningful engagements hits home, you'll first want to examine your balances regarding vacation and vocation. When energies get skewed too far in either direction, we feel discomfort. I recently heard a man talk about entering retirement with a plan of dividing his time into quarters: one quarter play, one quarter volunteering, one quarter family and friends, and one quarter learning and self-improvement. This actually sounds to me like a healthy leaning into retirement, but what he found is that events don't always comply with our intentions.

Within six months he found that his volunteering was taking over his life and squeezing the other areas out, which was creating a new form of imbalance and dissatisfaction. He had to learn to start saying no because it became clear that when nonprofits find a willing soul, they come running.

I've talked to others whose intention was to spend lots of time with family, but the family wasn't seeking the same level of engagement they were—these retirees soon began to feel they were imposing and intruding. Others found that once they left work, their social network crumbled, and they were lacking the enthusiasm for creating new networks. This, too, is a delicate balance (social and alone time) that has serious health implications. Recent research has demonstrated that loneliness is a predictor of various health issues.[6]

The Balance Sheet

Michael Finke, a retirement lifestyle expert at The American College has conducted extensive research on the factors that most influence satisfaction in retirement. He says the findings can be crystalized into three pillars: money, health, and connectivity.[7] You'll want to make sure you're experiencing well-being in all three categories.

Financially, there's a fine balance between spending too much and being afraid to spend at all. Many habitual savers struggle to enjoy their money after years of forcing themselves to squirrel away as much as possible. Health, in many respects, is impacted by how sedentary our lifestyle has become and how meaningful our engagements are. Social balance is just as important as connectivity and predicts satisfaction in this stage of life.

Rate yourself in the following areas, and ask yourself what you might alter in the areas where your balance feels a bit off.

Meaningful engagements	1 2 3 4 5 6 7 8 9 10	Play time
Time alone	1 2 3 4 5 6 7 8 9 10	Time with others
Sitting around	1 2 3 4 5 6 7 8 9 10	Being active
Spending too much	1 2 3 4 5 6 7 8 9 10	Afraid to spend

Forced or Phased?

If you are still working for others, I encourage you to begin discussions with your employers about a friendlier posture and attitude toward phased retirements instead of the heretofore one-and-done approach, which isn't healthy for most.

According to the most recent research by the U.S. Government Accounting Office on Phased Retirements, there is still plenty of room for growth with corporations and institutions. The estimated percentage of Society for Human Resource Management Members with Formal Phased Retirement Programs are, by industry:

Education	12%
Utilities	10%
Consulting	7%
High tech	7%
All industries	5%[8]

Clearly these numbers should be higher when one looks at the desire of mature adults to extend their work life, a trend that the GAO states is sure to continue: "Increases in labor force participation by women ages 55 to 64 and by women and men age 65 and older were the primary contributors to the overall increased labor force participation among older workers. Men ages 55 to 64 kept their labor force participation relatively stable from 2005 to 2016."[9]

This report states the expectation that the labor force participation of those 65 and older will continue to increase and that mature workers will constitute a larger part of the workforce overall by 2024 as the population in general ages. But—and this is a big but—almost half of the members of the 50-plus working cohort said they felt forced to retire; the percentage of those who felt this way was higher for those who retired in their 50s than in their 60s.

That being said, as the cohort aged, slightly more respondents said they wanted to retire when they did than said they felt forced to retire. The prior version of this study had reported the view that individuals approaching retirement tended to overestimate their ability to keep working past retirement age and often have to retire for reasons they did not anticipate, such as health problems, changes at their workplace, or caregiving responsibilities.

What does this mean to you? It means that the desire to work longer must be taken in the context of life in general. If you are in good health, if your workplace does have a phased retirement policy or attitude, and if you're not in a caregiving position, then you can start projecting your date out later. If these three factors are not germane to your situation, then you'll need to rethink your retirement timing.

Advocates Needed

Our societies are in need of advocates for the phased retirement approach, both formal and informal. Formal phased retirements are employer-based programs in which older workers can reduce their working hours in order to transition into retirement. This phased retirement may include partial drawdown of defined contribution or defined benefit pension benefits and a knowledge-transfer component, and the program may include health coverage for participants.

Informal phased retirement arrangements are not part of a formal program but are alternative methods to ease into retirement with the same employer, such as an ad hoc agreement or retirement followed by a term as a contractor. These approaches respectfully consider knowledge retention, skills transfer, workforce planning, and retirement planning. Employers who adopt a phased retirement posture as a human resource value-add not only retain workers with essential skills or knowledge, but also provide an incentive for other workers to retire. Workers who've been given this opportunity find phased retirement to be a much more positive way to ease into retirement.

If you are in a position to influence your organization's policies regarding phased retirement (or if you wish to approach your employer about a phased retirement for yourself), here are some short talking points you can use that speak to the advantages of a phased retirement program:

Worker retention: Seven of the nine employers interviewed in the GAO study suggested that allowing knowledgeable, experienced workers to phase into retirement often means they will stay longer with their employer. One employer said the reason they were very satisfied with the phased retirement program was that it helped them to retain highly educated and highly specialized workers. Another employer stated they appreciated the value of their workforce and if these employees were not participating in phased retirement, they would have been, most likely, already retired.

Knowledge transfer: Employers reported that maintaining the company knowledge base was critical. Many smaller employers recognize that their main challenge is the aging of the workforce and succession. In companies that have phased retirement programs, it is expected that the phasing worker will train and mentor his or her replacement, thus maintaining the company knowledge base. Some employers say that knowledge transfer is a chief objective of their phased retirement program, and it is left to key workers to create and implement a transfer plan.

Positive transition: Two-thirds of employers interviewed said providing a gradual pathway to retirement allows both employer and worker to adjust. One company noted that a phased retirement approach eased the transition for workers afraid of losing their sense of professional belonging as they transitioned away from paid work. This approach is not only an attractive off-ramp but is also a dignified way of rewarding employees for their years of service. Many companies find this to be more consistent with their organization's stated culture to provide a softer landing for valuable contributors.

Planning for the future: The majority of participating companies said that knowing when workers will retire allows employers to plan better for the future. A major goal of phased retirement is to help organizations with workforce planning by encouraging workers to let the company know about their retirement plans and to help transfer their knowledge before they fully retire, thus preventing brain drain.

Let's pull the curtain on the retirement leap and begin the healthier lean into our futures.

It's good for you, it's good for business … and it's good for the health of the retiring population.

CHAPTER 4

The New IRA: Individual Retirement Attitude

I used to get upset when a star player of our local team would take a big contract and head elsewhere to play. "No team loyalty anymore," I thought. After I was ceremoniously dismissed from my company after three decades, I realized why they do it. There's no team loyalty on the other side of the equation either. If you assume someone else has your best interests at heart, you assume wrongly.

—A "retired" sports fan

All one has to do to get in touch with the modern economic realities of retirement is to take a look at the trend of the past two decades away from the paternalistic pension approach toward the autonomy of defined contribution (DC) plans including 401(k) or 403(b). Pensions—also known as defined benefit (DB) plans—were originally designed to provide guaranteed benefits for the rest of your life, and in some cases, for the rest of your spouse's life. The percentage of people being covered by pension plans has been shrinking since 2000: as of 2018, 77% of employees in the public sector had pension plans (compared to 81% five years ago) while only 13% in the private sector had them (compared to 21% five years ago).[1] But the migration from pensions to self-directed plans has already begun in the public sector and will be a massive trend going forward as more and more states and municipalities struggle to meet their pension liabilities.

The chief difference between a defined benefit and a defined contribution plan is who is on the hook of responsibility. Organizations are sending a clear message that they are not interested in being on that hook any longer. For decades, workers were like passengers on the retirement bus, leaving the driving and benefits planning to organizations. Today, however, we are being put behind the wheel of our own retirement savings vehicle and told to drive. What happens on the road ahead is entirely up to us.

Many DC plans originally came about because companies were failing and couldn't meet their pension obligations, but today's companies are doing away with pension programs for other reasons, most of which are related to sustainability. These days, even financially stable firms are doing away with pension plans. Employers like DC plans because they are cheaper to maintain while employees like them because they are portable. In the days when pensions proliferated, people were afraid to walk away from careers they found unsatisfying for fear of losing the pension benefits that could sustain them for many decades. Today, without such pensions in place, most people can simply transfer their DC accounts into an individual retirement account (IRA) and portage their career efforts to other streams.

There has never been a more serious need for people to take responsibility for themselves and their own retirements. Many of the pensions that still exist are seriously underfunded. According to the Pew Charitable Trusts, state pension plans had a deficit of $1.4 trillion, as of 2016 (the latest data available).[2] This massive amount is nothing more than hidden debt, representing an obligation owed where the promising party no longer has the resources to meet its obligations. For years I have written that the proper definition of a pension is "a promise that is good until it's not."

A closer look at the obligations assumed by the Pension Benefit Guaranty Corporation (PBGC) should give us all pause. The PBGC assumed the pension obligations of a number of failed airlines' pensions as well as those of steel companies and auto manufacturers. The Pension Benefit Guaranty Corporation paid $153 million in financial assistance to 81 insolvent multiemployer plans in FY'18 alone. The program is expected to run out of money if new legislation isn't enacted. The single-payer program is in better shape, but combined the program appears to be $51.5 billion in the red.[3]

Also bear in mind that the PGBC is the party guaranteeing the benefits of failed institutions. More corporate pensions will fail in the next decade, as will many of those of states and large cities.

The pension world is following a more Anglo-Saxon approach. More individualism, take care of yourself, not your neighbor.
                                        —European employer

The reasons the private sector has largely done away with pension plans are manifold but include the fact that companies disliked having to report their actuarial soundness to the Department of Labor (there were penal fees for not reporting). This lack of reporting—as well as turning a blind eye toward critical information such as long-term perspectives on plan funding—is a critical factor in contributing to the underfunding of pension plans. Additional accounting hanky-panky comes into play when corporations often state pension benefits as assets, and use those assets to balance their budgets in order to stay in business. As absurd as it sounds, accounting rules allow firms to list those benefits as assets even when the firm is severely underfunded toward meeting those obligations.

On the public pension side of the matter, there are political drivers to blame for long-term insolvency in many of these public pensions. DB plans are funded by means of cyclical resources, meaning you would expect additional funding when times are good and possible cutbacks in funding when resources are scarce, but elected officials tend to cut pension funding when the markets are good and cut back on pension funding when markets are bad to balance budgets. Only politicians could come up with such an ingenious plan for hastening insolvency!

The developing scenario around public pension obligations will emerge as a major concern for taxpayers in the coming years. Half of the state pensions in America are funded to only 70% or less. Forbes called underfunded public pensions the "next great retirement crisis."[4] Many state and local governments are following the acts of failing pension plans—like those of the airline industry—where market values of pension fund assets and liabilities are off the balance sheet (Statement of Net Assets) of state and local governments, which only delays the inevitable. Pensions are like bonds in that they are obligations to pay. When the entity cannot pay, they raise taxes or cut back on programs that currently benefit their employees.

My goal is not to paint a bleak portrait of the future but to prepare you for what lies ahead. The irreversible conclusion is that the onus is now squarely upon each and every one of us to assume responsibility for every aspect of our economic well-being. Some people make the argument that much of the European debt crisis can be traced to institutional obligations that were never realistic. Europeans who planned on retiring with full benefits at 58 years of age are now busy making other plans.[5] My point is this: no one can afford to sit around expecting an institution to follow through on promises they have made, corporations and governments included. Some of the reality checks of this modern age are as follows:

- If you have a pension, assume that benefit erosion will continue.
- Assume you will work longer.
- Assume you will live longer.
- Assume that there will be unplanned challenges, both financial and nonfinancial.

Here's my definition of the IRA. It is actually an *Individual Retirement Attitude*. I can no longer assume that any institution has my best interests at heart, and I will assume total responsibility for my fiscal well-being. I will plan on not only living longer but working longer as well, and I will be highly selective about the work I choose. I will remain flexible in my approach, as I know there will be surprises and challenges in the journey ahead.

Assume You Will Work Longer

We'll talk about this throughout this book. If indeed we buy into the idea that 65 is the new 55, or 45, or whatever chronological marker you choose, it also stands to reason that 65 would not necessarily be the date of extraction from the workforce. With ageist biases prevalent in many organizational settings, the pursuit and extension of work in your 60s and even early 70s will not be without its challenges. Maintaining relevance and up-to-speed aptitude in the modern workplace is the theme of Chapter 9.

Assume You Will Live Longer

How long should you plan on living? Should you consult an actuarial table or a longevity expert? I would recommend going with the expert—a recent study indicates that that expert is you! The study explores Subjective Life Expectancy (SLE), a model where "individuals take into account their own age-related actuarial probabilities of life expectancy, but also consider other autobiographical details including factors such as their parents' longevity and their own lifestyles and health."[6] In other words, we know ourselves better than anyone else. The research concluded that though the idea of SLE is a relatively new concept for research, there is enough evidence to conclude that self-estimates of life expectancy are reasonably accurate.

How long you expect to live has an important bearing on many of your "third stage of life" decisions—retirement being one of the first and foremost. Changes in Western societies demographically, economically, and socially have worked to form novel patterns for retirement. Staged or bridged retirements are becoming more common. Because of the confluence of increased longevity, the gradual eradication of mandatory retirement policies, and the macro shift toward personal financial responsibility in retirement, we will see these bridged retirements grow ever longer.

So, based on your family DNA and your personal health habits/lifestyle, what is your best estimate for longevity? Your guess is as good as the actuarial experts. If you believe your expectancy to be 87, you can work backwards from that number with regard to both your financial and life satisfaction needs and begin to plot out your individual retirement path. SLE allows you to design your own time frame for how you will transition through retirement, as well as how you will plan the distribution of your finances through the various stages, which was coined by a certified financial planner named Michael K. Stein as go-go, slow-go, and no-go.[7]

Ask yourself the following questions:

- How old do I feel versus my actual age?
- What is my optimum "work until" age?
- What has been my parents'/grandparents' average longevity?
- How would I rate my dietary, physical fitness, and intellectual growth overall on a 1–10 scale?

From your answers to these questions, you can make a guesstimate at your own life expectancy. And keep in mind that how long you decide to work can have a bearing on this number as well. It would stand to reason that those who expect to live longer would also plan to retire later. A study by van Solinge and Henkens supported this assumption, showing that "Subjective Life Expectancy was a significant predictor of intended retirement age, even after controlling for important demographic factors such as gender, age, income, education, health, marital status, and family longevity."[8]

Another study by von Bonsdorff, Shultz, Leskinen, and Tansky found that those who expect to live longer may feel that they have time to engage in both work and nonwork activities. These people tend to see death as a far-off event relative to others of the same age. Because of this, they aren't ready to consider changing life priorities and retirement. They also concluded that those who have a high SLE are "likely to be contemplating a long retirement period with lots of opportunities for activity," and consequently will sense the need to be engaged in paid work for a longer period in order to be able to pay for the retirement that they envision.[9]

On the flipside, those late career workers with a short SLE would be inclined to avoid considering negative information about the financial risks of early retirement and would opt to focus instead on activities like leisure and family togetherness. Either way, it is left to you.

The bottom line is that our mental/attitudinal approach is a significant factor in this stage of life. Research results indicate that late career workers and retirees have "developed a mental model of their own likely life expectancy, and this mental model influenced decisions that have important consequences both for their personal circumstances as well as for organizations managing projected skill shortages and for governments planning for the social security of older people."[10]

As individuals, we are in charge of our own destinies more than we think. While there will always be unexpected, accidental, and unavoidable events, we're all better off determining our own paths instead of leaving the journey to institutions.

Assume That There Will Be Improvisational Challenges

As stated earlier, because it takes time for us to adjust both psychologically and financially to full retirement, bridges or transitions in and out of work have become more common. Postretirement bridge employment has positive implications for those organizations that seek to maintain talent and knowledge. In addition to the obvious financial gains, it also has physical and mental health benefits for us as individuals.

There are many already-retired persons who have returned to paid bridge employment. For over a decade there has been a growing body of research demonstrating that those who leave retirement to reenter the workforce have more positive attitudes to their preretirement work and are in better health. In other words, they feel healthy—both in body and spirit—and they know that by being engaged, they will extend that good health.

Chances are, if you attempt full retirement, you won't get it right the first time. As we've already discussed, it can take most of us two to four attempts to find the exact balance of the vocation and vacation we are searching for. It also takes time to find the proper balance between spending and saving. More time in play equals more spent and less earned.

Not surprisingly, two of the chief financial motivators for people who are engaged in bridge employment in their 60s and 70s are (1) medical health insurance and (2) being able to continue contributing to a workplace retirement plan, both of which increase in importance as we age.[11] Many of us, when considering inflationary health coverage and health care costs, decide that it is worth working longer to maintain coverage. Many of us want to delay distributions of our 401(k) plans, and so we continue to work and build those assets.

In the long run there are two balances you are challenged with finding on an individual level: working and playing and spending and saving. Allow yourself a practice run or two to find the balance you need. It is no longer necessary to think of retirement as a cliff to jump from (which is why people wanted parachutes) but as an uncharted road where you will need to advance carefully and map out what you like and don't like. There will be bridges in and out of employment, volunteer engagements, and more.

Consequently, modern retirement is a bit like an improvisational stage of life where you'll be deciding to go in and out of work and other interests based on how you feel at the time and how well balanced your current lifestyle feels to you. "Have fun with it" are the words of one practice-run retiree in her 70s who decided to leave the corporate world behind in her late 50s, start her own retail business, and dabble in a number of different ventures.

As you age and meet the improvisational challenges of this stage of life, you will find many that have blazed the trail ahead of you saying that "It is more about attitude than anything else." What is the healthiest outlook you can take into the next stage of life? The following are essential:

- I will be a driver and not a passenger. I will assume responsibility for my own well-being, financially and otherwise.
- I will respond instead of despond. I'm going to make the most of the situation I am in. If I need to go back to work, I'm going to look for work that has social and intellectual benefits.
- I will thrive, not just survive. With all the wisdom and experience I have gathered, I know what matters and what doesn't. I will apply that wisdom and direct my efforts in the most meaningful ways possible.

Viktor Frankl once wrote about the relationship between "position" and "disposition" and how understanding this distinction can make a difference in our lives.[12] The difference, he taught, is that one state—position—is the situation we find ourselves in. We may not have planned it this way, but here we are. We now have a choice about how to respond to this position, with our disposition. Some choose to become bitter, dismayed, and angry that things didn't go according to plan. Others choose to take a position to enjoy the adventure of it all, rise to the challenges, explore new avenues, and revel in the novelty of new paths. Frankl taught that the "position taken" is far more important than the position you find yourself in at the moment. This, in a nutshell, is what attitude is all about: figure out what position you are in, and determine what position you will take!

Boredom Isn't on Anyone's Bucket List

I met Fred when he was 80 years old; he looked and comported himself like a man 20 years his junior. At the time, he was running a nonprofit organization and working six- to eight-hour days. It was obvious in talking to him that retirement was an option he could choose any time he wanted—he just didn't want to. I asked what it was about retirement that failed to attract him.

Fred told me about turning 65 and how all his close friends moved en masse to Palm Springs—the "last stop," he called it—to take up a life of retirement leisure. "They invited me out to sell me on the lifestyle, and so I went to see for myself. We sat down for cocktails before dinner, and each of them went around and told me about their golf match or tennis match, stroke by stroke. The next year they invited me out again and told me they were going to 'close the deal' with me. We sat down for cocktails somewhat earlier than last year, and they went around the table one by one and told me about their golf and tennis matches, stroke by stroke." He paused and then said, "And that's when I knew it."

Fred had me, and so I asked, "Knew what?"

"First, you're bored—then you're boring. I never want to be that boring."

I laughed uproariously at his candor and incisiveness. I'd never heard anything like it, but I'll never forget how convincing he was as a relevant force at the age of 80. He instantly became one of my *retirementors* (I'll introduce more retirementors throughout the book). I want to have that kind of balance and relevance in my life as long as I possibly can. I love to play as much as the next guy, but I don't want to bore people with stories and accounts that put them to sleep because playing is all I do.

Boredom is the result of:

- Loss of challenge (not enough to do)
- Loss of intrigue (no longer curious)
- Isolation and loneliness (no longer connecting with others)
- Loss of identity (no longer feeling useful)

When too much capacity meets too little opportunity, boredom ensues.

I always find it a bit humorous when I hear people saying, "I don't know how I ever had time to work; I'm so busy now." As long as the busyness is enjoyable and engaging for these people, I'm happy for them. But when their answer is "I'm keeping busy," I often like to dig a little deeper and ask, "Busy doing what?"

Being "busy" can be overrated. What are you busy doing? As the author Mary O'Connor put it, "It's not so much how busy you are but why you are busy. The bee is praised. The mosquito is swatted."

Monotone Living

Monotony is a predictor of boredom. If you do the same thing every day with the same people, at the same place, at the same time, with the same result, it's just a matter of time before reality sets in and every day becomes the same. That's not quite living up to the promise that, in retirement, "every day is Saturday."

I remember being driven to an event in Missouri where I was scheduled to speak, and talking with the driver about what it was that caused him to want to drive part time. He was just a year into his retirement.

He told me: "There was a group of five of us that all retired about the same time. We would meet every morning for breakfast, then head to the golf course and play the same way we did the day before. The stories that we told were constantly retold. The lines that were used were reused. After six months of this conversational carousel, I had to do something else. Ironically, all five of us now are working part time. Now when we get together, it's more fun and refreshing."

How You're Wired

Robert Delamontagne, PhD, author of *The Retiring Mind: How to Make the Psychological Transition to Retirement,* noted that he was surprised to find that he felt bored and aimless almost immediately after retiring from a highly competitive career as a software company executive. In his research he found that people with certain personality characteristics like competitiveness and assertiveness had more difficulty adjusting than say, mild-mannered persons who had careers in lower-pressure jobs. According to Delamontagne, "The very attributes that make people successful in their work life often work against them in retirement."

Pay attention to how you're wired because it's a reliable predictor of whether you will either flourish or flounder in retirement. Another man or woman's experience will not necessarily inform yours. That's why the *Individual Retirement Attitude* is so important—because it's your well-being that's on the line. If you're an adrenaline-driven achiever, don't expect the fuse to blow out on that aspect of your being the day you turn 65. In Chapter 11, "Redefining *You*: What's Your Retirementality?" you'll find a profile to help you begin the process of realizing how you're wired, especially as it pertains to retiring.

When Frustration Replaces Fascination

The other night I heard a statement on retirement I thought I would never hear. The opinion came from Derrick, locally famous for his obsession with golf. He retired in his mid-50s with a platinum parachute from a Fortune 100 company, managed his money well, and jumped immediately on his hobbyhorse and rode. He built a mini golf clinic in his basement where he would try out the latest gizmos purchased from infomercials, and practice his swing on winter days when he wasn't out West or down South actually playing the game. During the Minnesota golf season he could be seen at the range and on the course almost every single day.

At the range he is a study in experimentation on his idée fixe, constantly tweaking, fine-tuning, and methodically repeating motions to ingrain them into his motor memory. This has been a constant pattern in his life for the past four years.

Recently, he sat down next to me at a public event and confided in me, "I'm playing too much. I've got to do something more with my life. I think I can actually help some people."

Derrick's retirement plans had been hit with the law of diminishing returns. He didn't mention it at this moment, but I had seen the pattern evolving. In his first year or two of retirement, his golf game really improved, but as the love of the game grew from passionate to obsessive his game began to erode. By year four it had become a pivotal point of frustration in his life, hence his change of heart.

Over the past few years I had broached the topic of working or volunteering in retirement and the need for keeping some sort of purpose-driven activity, but he would brightly respond that his dream was playing itself out exactly as planned. The realization came later to Derrick than it does to many retirees that one can't squeeze lifeblood from a rock—humans simply weren't designed for lives centered exclusively on leisure. I use golf as an example again here because it's a commonly romanticized existence for many retirees, but one can easily substitute another sport, hobby, or pastime. As with any pursuit, too much can become monotonous.

Realistic Expectations

Many retirees' lives are literally on the rocks—both existentially and dietarily—because of the false expectations set up for them (or by them) in retirement. There are three mythical nirvanas that people strive for in retirement only to later awaken to empty, banal, and unimaginative realities:

> *This part of life is going to be about me.* This is a formula for emptiness.

I am going to surround myself with people just like me. This is a formula for stagnation.

I am going to do nothing but relax. This is a formula for listlessness.

This Part of Life Is Going to Be about Me

A weekly schedule that includes time only for yourself is like charting a course bound for desolation of soul and spirit. Humans are designed in such a way that there needs to be some sense of higher purpose—of bringing value to others—in order to feel fulfillment in life. Many retirees get it right and schedule plenty of time in their lives that is about others: spending time with their grandchildren, helping their children, and volunteering with local causes. Those who pursue agendas that are exclusively me-centered find themselves enjoying life less each week. Such a lifestyle can be an open portal to depression and illness, as well.

I Am Going to Surround Myself with People Like Me

I don't think I'm going out on a limb when I predict that the next generation of retirees—if that word is still even used—will opt out of the closed community concept. Recently, a friend told me about his experience when taking his teenage children to see their grandparents at an exclusive retirement community. They were on pins and needles the entire time because the codes strictly stated what children could and could not do on the premises. Everywhere they went there were septuagenarian spies stationed, ready to report potential violations of hot-tub or hallway policies. Really? This is the life you dreamed of? A life of hiding behind walls and not allowing anyone younger than 55 near the gates?

When we quarantine our lives to be with only those who are similar to us and purposely exclude the young and diverse, we are scripting our lives into total stagnation. Our existences become like the movie *Groundhog Day*: every day is exactly like the last, and we don't know how to break out of the monotony. Progress is stymied in our personal lives when we cloister ourselves away from the world. And we must never forget that once we become bored, we soon become boring.

After giving a speech on successful aging, I was approached by a man in his 60s who said, "I have to tell you about my father." He went on to tell me how his father, at his 70th birthday celebration, stood up and told all in attendance, "I have an announcement to make ... I'm going to start hanging out with younger people. All my friends are getting sick, and some are dying." And he did. He started engaging in hobbies where his fellow participants were in their 30s, 40s, and 50s. This gentleman ended the story by informing me that when his father passed away at 99, his funeral was full of people 30 years younger and more. I could tell by the glint in his eye that his father's example had truly inspired those around him.

I Am Going to Do Nothing but Relax

Shakespeare said, "Leisure is a beautiful garment for a day but a horrible choice for permanent attire."

Ennui is a guarantee when sitting around is the whole agenda. I would go further and say that the garment of leisure begins to stink the longer it is worn. The grumpy old guy on the tennis court, the couple competing to get to the shore first and gather sea shells, the woman with nothing to do but provoke condo-association warfare, the foursome who spends all afternoon sipping cocktails, all speak of the unflattering aroma of a life centered exclusively on leisure.

A gerontologist at the Mayo Clinic once told me, "A life of total ease is two steps removed from a life of total disease. First step is that they get bored, the second step is that they grow pessimistic, and finally they get ill."

Perhaps you have witnessed this type of existential descent with a retiree close to you. The simple fact of the matter is that leisure cannot and never will be able to pay us what we need as humans to feel that our existence matters. We all need purpose and we all need progress—and age is irrelevant in this regard.

Me-centric lifestyles painted into tight circles, with leisure at the core, are destined to experience the law of diminishing returns. The kind of retirement lifestyle that pays perpetual dividends is where "me" is balanced with others, circles of close friends are balanced with exploration on the peripheries, and leisure is balanced with work that brings value to others and meaning to yourself. The greatest decision a retiree makes is not how they invest their assets but how they invest their life.

For Better or Worse but *Not* for Lunch

According to Pew Research Center, from 1990 to 2015, divorce rates for those over 50 years of age have gone up by 109%.[1] A financial planner in New Jersey told me that one of the most heartbreaking scenarios that kept repeating in his planning practice was the number of clients divorcing after retirement. He talked about how discouraging it was to spend years assisting these couples whom he had grown quite fond of, only to see them break apart after retirement—because the lifestyle was not what they had planned for. The lesson is that personal space is required for relationships to last and couples can have a hard time in the retirement transition. This planner told me that as a preemptive move to prepare them for the transition, he had started sending the book you are reading a year ahead of their proposed retirement dates.

My mother-in-law preempted any such development in her marriage when she sat down with her husband on the first day of his retirement from teaching for 42 years and asked him to sign a document she had drafted, called "The Pre-retirement Agreement." The agreement was literally prenup-meets-retirement! One woman in Texas put it to me this way: "I've got twice the husband, half the space—and he's getting bigger." It's hard to top that description, and I know it resonates with a lot of spouses.

Losing Your Identity

My friend Larry told me about a friend of his who was the envy of his peers when he took full retirement at age 55 and headed to Florida to pursue a life of seven-days-a-week leisure. After serendipitously running into his old pal seven years later, he said to me, "We're exactly the same age, but to look at us you'd swear there were 15 years between us—my friend being on the not-so-flattering end of the comparison." This man had been a mover and shaker in his industry and complained that now "he couldn't get a plumber to show up, and felt he had been moved from 'Who's who' to 'Who's he?'"

Role transitions theory purports that one's identification with pre-retirement employment roles will affect postretirement adjustment.[2] Maintenance of an individual's identity through the retirement process will lead to a better sense of well-being. Depending on the level of stress the pre-retirement role caused, role transitions can be experienced as either a relief or a loss.[3] Drinking can therefore increase or decrease, depending on whether alcohol use is associated with work-oriented social roles or whether alcohol is used to cope with role loss.

One study explored the impact of voluntariness of retirement—whether it was the individual's decision at the time—as a factor of retirement's impact on health outcomes. The authors concluded that both voluntary and involuntary retirees may use alcohol to cope with the stress of sudden change in their employment status.[4] High pre-retirement job satisfaction, involuntary retirement, and pre-retirement workplace stress are all risk factors for higher consumption of alcohol and a greater likelihood of alcohol problems. As we discussed earlier, retirement for many can mean diminished breadth of social roles, which can lead to discouragement. On the other side, individuals whose social circles increase during retirement may be at risk for problem drinking if those social influences are permissive of drinking.

The Rearview Mirror

In a *New York Times* "Workologist" column, I read an interesting inquiry from a retired 55-year-old male reader who had recently sold his business for a great profit. Financially, he felt he was extremely well set. He wrote, "While the idea of an early retirement was always appealing, I'm finding that I'm bored out of my mind. I miss the activity and satisfaction that came from building and running a company. I don't feel I can talk to any of my friends about this, as they are hard at work and can't really identify with my boredom."[5]

On the flipside, this gentleman felt he might be too old to reenter a workplace that was catering to Millennials, and after 25 years of autonomy and calling his own shots, he had understandable reservations regarding reporting to someone else. The question he posed to the columnist is one I encounter quite often: "Is this something I need to get over, and just enjoy the fruits of my labor, or should I try to reenter the workforce in some limited capacity?"

Like this retired businessman, many of us walk into retirement with rose-colored glasses and naïveté regarding the impact on our emotional, social, intellectual, and spiritual beings. We must enter this stage of life with our eyes wide open to the dangers, pitfalls, and traps that swallow many whole—and from which many never return.

How do you avoid the deleterious impacts of boredom in retirement? How can you and your friends avoid the undesirable condition of retirement whiplash, where the reality catches up with you suddenly? I suggest having a conversation with a good friend, a retirement coach, or even a career counselor about work, intellectual capital, and all the things you do to fuel personal esteem and expression.

Age has nothing to do with it. What you bring to the game and how long you want to play is what matters. There's nothing wrong with going from being a starting player to a supporting player in the next phase of life, as long as you are somehow, in some way, invested in the game of life. If you have the need to feel useful, don't get trapped into a life that feels useless to you. Everyone is wired differently in this respect. Follow your own wiring and not the diagram that the world at large advises for you. You won't be disappointed . . . and you won't be bored!

A New Mind-Set: Retire on Purpose

Too many people die with their music still in them.
—Oliver Wendell Holmes

I have seen too many retirees adrift on a sea of aimlessness, boredom, and discontentment. They found freedom from their old job and the old routines but didn't sufficiently contemplate what that freedom could lead them toward. There is an entire generation of people arising who have decided to make their "second life" of life the most meaningful one. This group understands the habits, attitudes, and pursuits that directly correlate with successful aging and staying young at heart. Words like *curiosity*, *connectivity*, *challenge*, and *contributing* are hallmarks of a new generation of retirees, who are transforming "retiring" into "refiring" and "reclining" into "refining." These people are leaving an indelible impact on the people, ideas, and causes they care about the most.

In an excellent *The Atlantic* article titled, *Making Aging Positive*, Linda Fried, one of the founders of the Experience Corps, stated, "The truth is that we have created a new stage of life but have not yet envisioned its purpose, meaning, and opportunities, and the space is being filled with our fears. Like a drunk searching for a lost wallet under the wrong lamppost 'because that's where the light is,' we are not looking for answers in the right places."[1] Fried is correct, as is her prognosis of what it will take to change the problem: "We don't yet know what this new stage of life can be, but the first step is to change the lens through which we view aging and challenge our stereotypical assumptions."[2]

Famed psychologists Erik and Joan Erikson viewed later life as a time when the impulse to give back to society (generativity) becomes an urgent need. Carl Jung, who was rather prescient among early psychologists in his interest in the challenges of the second half of life, saw older age as a rich period of spiritual growth and individuation.

Activist Betty Friedan, who trained as a social psychologist, researched the issue of aging late in her life, and suggested that there is a "fountain of age"—a period of renewal, growth, and experimentation based on a new freedom.

Having a strong sense of purpose impacts us at every level of our health: physically, mentally, and spiritually. In the last decade we have learned from scientific studies in medicine, neuroscience, and psychology that living purposefully has measurable effects on health outcomes. Living purposefully makes you 52% less likely to develop Alzheimer's, prevents strokes by as much as 44%, and reduces the chances of a cardiovascular event by 19%. And these are just a few of the physical impacts.[3] We've got to adjust our thinking about what is possible past 60 because, in the recent past, we have been misled on this matter.

We now know that exercise can significantly increase muscle mass in older adults, even among nursing home residents. We now understand that physical and mental exercise can enhance the brain's plasticity; and we now realize that meaningful social engagement and activity can reduce the risk of social isolation, depression, and illness while enabling us to make a difference in our society.

This chapter is all about that exploration and the attitudes necessary to harvest the best life possible with the years we have. As we enter our "second life," the attitude we choose will have the greatest bearing on our fate. We are entering the final stages of a retirement revolution.

Without question, for the past 15–20 years the institution of retirement has been morphing into something other than what we are familiar with. The idea has been evolving slowly toward something other than a playground agenda for senior citizens. The revolution taking place is that many are seeing this stage of life as just the opposite—*the most fertile period of life for meaningful pursuit.*

The population of experienced adults could be divided into a set of attitudes toward this particular phase of life:

- The "I'm done" crowd
- The "I have to" crowd
- The "I'm inspired" crowd

"I'm Done"

I can sympathize with those of you who have suffered through years of soul-crushing work with little satisfaction, or corporate environments rife with selfishness, sabotage, and subterfuge. You have had enough and just want to trade in your business suit for jeans and a T-shirt. As detailed in earlier chapters, you may be in for some unexpected surprises regarding the vacuum that remains when you cease making any sort of meaningful contribution. This attitude is based on the premise of "I've earned this"—and you have. The future is yours to mold; just make sure you're not the one that is being molded.

"I Have To"

Those of you who have adopted this stance toward your circumstances have had your plans disrupted. Whether it was the disappointment of a time of unemployment, stock market losses, or recession period realities affecting your career, when you say, "I'm working because I have to," you are telling the truth. However, this truth need not be a death march. For every mature worker I meet who has adopted the obligatory attitude, I meet another with a grateful outlook who says, "Hey, things didn't work out according to plan, but thankfully I'm still healthy enough to work and I'm earning an income. I've learned to see the best in these circumstances."

It is attitude that makes a life, not vice versa. More important than the circumstance we face is the disposition we choose to have toward that circumstance. In *The Doctor and the Soul,* Viktor Frankl wrote that in life we have a position (how and where we came to be), a destiny (what has happened), and a disposition (how we choose to respond to our "how and where" and "what has happened"). It is the disposition, or the "position taken," that ultimately defines the individual's life, not what happens and why.[4]

Ask a cynic why he is a cynic and he will tell you it is because of his position and destiny—what happened and why it happened. Cynics have chosen the worst possible disposition: to give up on the possibilities because their rose garden may have contained some weeds. The all-important point cynics miss is that their disposition has deepened their unwanted position and entrenched them in a destiny they loathe. Your attitude—your "position taken"—toward events is what defines you, not the events.

"I'm Inspired"

This is the true joy of life: the being used up for a purpose, recognized by yourself as a mighty one: being a force of nature instead of a feverish, selfish, little clot of ailments and grievances, complaining that the world will not devote itself to making you happy.
—George Bernard Shaw

This contingent has decided to "retire on purpose"—whether they have to work or choose to be engaged, paid, or unpaid. If you are part of the "I'm inspired" crowd, you are pursuing meaningful work with a paycheck attached or perhaps getting compensated spiritually or emotionally. Your stories are the accounts the rest of us can draw upon for personal inspiration and guidance. You are paving a path of hopefulness and fulfillment for those of us who have yet to encounter this phase. Your stories, along with others' individual retirement stories, will reshape this planet as people begin to realize the revolutionary retirement attitude that changes everything: *I can make a difference now like never before.*

Why now more than ever before? Because you have experience. Because you know what works and what doesn't. Because you have clarity of what energizes your soul and what enervates it. As a result of my work, I have been blessed over the past two decades to meet many such retirementors—their stories, vision, resilience, resourcefulness, and buoyant attitudes never fail to inspire me.

Just as I was writing this, I had a chance encounter on the driving range with a retired physician from the Mayo clinic. I knew he had read this book a couple of years ago when he chose retirement. He approached me and said, "Well, Mitch, I'm not in the game but I'm not in the bleachers, either. I'm not the water boy making a new kind of contribution." I asked him to explain.

He went on to tell me an account the likes of which I had never heard before: " I approached a limo company that drives a lot of patients from the Minneapolis airport to the Mayo Clinic and told them I'd drive for them, but I wanted to drive only patients. These incoming patients have a lot of anxiety which I'm able to help placate if we fall into a conversation. The patients going back to the airport after their clinic visit often have many questions and concerns as well, which I can lend some insights and reassurances toward as well."

"Have you ever picked up one of your former patients?" I asked him. "Yes," he replied, "and they look at me shocked and say, 'Doctor B!' to which I reply, 'Today I am your driver.'"

I can't begin to express my admiration for the humility and compassion this "retired" physician is demonstrating. I don't know many former doctors who would allow themselves to volunteer as a driver. He's making a significant contribution!

My own father's attitude fits this description. As I write this, he is approaching his 84th birthday and still manages the syndication for *The Daily Dose*, my radio feature heard on close to 150 stations around the country. I created these 90-second "attitude adjustments" to counter the unending flow of rants and politically infused railing that seem to dominate the airwaves.

Dad spent almost 30 years as a sports journalist in radio and television before switching to a sales career that lasted another 20 years. Twenty-two years ago I asked him if he would take on the syndication work for my program, and he's still pounding the phones every morning. The work is not for the faint of heart. He hears 100 "nos" for every "yes," but he persists through the drought periods, and we're always thrilled when a new market jumps on board. Because of his resilience and indefatigable efforts, hundreds of thousands of listeners around the country get a dose of inspiration to start their day. When I hear from listeners that they appreciate the program, I think of Dad's tireless efforts. He knows what these attitudinal arrows can mean to someone's day. He wouldn't tell you he's retired, because he's not. But he is semiretired *on purpose* and is grateful to be engaged.

I'd like to propose the following four attitudes that I have witnessed time and again in the lives of those 65-plus-year-olds that have caused them to flourish instead of flounder. Take the New Retirementality challenge and integrate these four attitudes into your own life:

1. Keep meaningful pursuit at the core.
2. Challenge your mind, body, and spirit.
3. Refuse to be defined by age.
4. Keep an eye on your "attitude instrument."

Meaningful Pursuits: A Midlife Crisis Gone Horribly Right

If we buy into the idea that we are to get and give the most we can from our lives, then retirement at any juncture has new meaning and possibilities. Every month I meet new examples of the New Retirementality—those who treat their lives as an evolving exploration mission. They are not content to sit around and watch television or simply bide their time with random busyness.

Marie Ens had served as a missionary to orphaned children and abandoned grandparents in Cambodia for 38 years when her denomination "invited her to retire at age 66." They wouldn't bend on their retirement policy. A year later she was celebrating her 67th birthday with her four children and grandchildren, and announced, "I'm 67, and nobody can tell me what to do with my life. I'm going back to Cambodia on my own to get back to my

mission." A side note: after her party ended, Marie went to the grocery store and heard Billy Joel singing "This is my life, leave me
alone" on the PA system. She took that as a message from God.

I asked Marie about her decision to return to Cambodia, and
she told me "You don't retire from a calling." Our family sponsors
two of the children in her home, and it's easy to understand how
Marie was unable to walk away from these precious charges.

When visiting Place of Rescue for the first time, one can easily
be drawn into thinking that this is an idyllic home—a place filled
with perfect children laughing and smiling grannies with wide
(almost toothless!) grins. But beneath the laughter and wide grins,
Place of Rescue is a haven, an oasis in a world that can be hard,
cold-hearted, and downright mean. The fact is that this is a place
where you encounter children who have overcome abandonment,
grandmothers who are alone after losing their mates in the killing
fields and their grown children to AIDS, and entire families who
live under the daily shadow of HIV/AIDS.

Marie is a retirementor: an inspirational example of the idea
that you don't have to be rich to live a rich life, and you can't
impose a retirement age on a heart full of purpose and meaningful
engagement.

The math of the New Retirementality includes calculating how
to best deploy financial assets—if we have any to share or spare—
and how to capitalize on all the assets of our persona and identity.
This is our social and soul capital and is, in my opinion, the next
great frontier for so-called "retirement planning": unifying the discussions of managing monetary and social assets. The discussions
we have been having about retirement have brought us to this
place but cannot take us from this place. It can no longer be simply
a "retirement" discussion, but instead must become a New Retirementality discussion that helps us all define our next act.

You don't have to go to Africa or Cambodia to live out your purpose, but it's helpful to be open to different possibilities. You may
find your purposeful engagement around the block, on the other
side of the world, or anywhere there is a need that stirs your heart
and suits your skills.

This purposeful approach is being recognized by AARP, which
provides five recipients $60,000 each to celebrate their achievements

and broaden the work they've done using life experiences to create a better world. Originally sponsored by Encore, past winners have included people who:

- Represented low-income homeowners in foreclosure.
- Brought safe drinking water to villages in India.
- Helped female parolees make a successful transition with job training, housing, and legal services.
- Taught life skills to low-income adults and teens.
- Brought seniors and foster care kids together to enrich each other's lives.

The Retiring on Purpose Profile

If you would like to think through your own purpose and direction, I encourage you to work through the *Retiring on Purpose* exercise that follows. This exercise will help you set your own direction and define the engagements that will be meaningful to you as you enter the third and potentially most promising stage of life.

Select five choices from the list below that best describe your next phase of life and place these on your (A) list. Place your second five choices on the (B) list.

Travel	Explore
Continue present work	Connect with friends
Dust off old dreams	Hang out with retired friends
Relax	Learn new skill
Find balance	Educate myself
Do consulting work	Help others
Teach others	Connect with family
Play	Work with charities
Increase my community involvement	Connect with a cause
Spend time with spouse	Help out with grandkids
Mentor others	Engage in a hobby
Work with charities	Connect with a cause
Engage in a hobby	Help out school kids
Get a part-time hobby job	Do projects at home

Take it easy	Take on a new challenge
Start a new business	Go back to school
Write about experiences	Build something

My A List:

1. _____
2. _____
3. _____
4. _____
5. _____

My B List:

1. _____
2. _____
3. _____
4. _____
5. _____

Exploration Agenda

Having exciting agendas on the horizon has the effect of infusing people with hope and a joy for living. The thrill of something new, encountering the unknown, and taking a risk should never grow old if we're viewing life with an exploratory eye. If you want to put some *P.E.P.* in your step—the Places, Experiences, and People you'd like to encounter—start an exploration agenda.

I remember the day I read about the passing of the aforementioned Dr. Frankl at 92 years of age—I had often fantasized about going to meet him somewhere he was speaking or even traveling to Austria if necessary. I used to tell myself I was going to do this someday but that someday had now passed. I was saddened by my own lack of courage or initiative to just simply do it. His work and writings have made—and continue to make—a profound mark in my life and work. I had read that he was very gracious about receiving visitors for a chat because he was deeply interested in what gave people meaning in their lives. But, alas, I had let this one slip.

I was fortunate enough to get an object lesson from my brother on the audacious pursuit of one's exploration agenda. We are both lifelong Boston Celtic fans and decided to fly to Boston to see a game. My brother is a guy who, in a charmingly pleasant manner, will not take "no" for an answer if he decides he wants to do something. I refer to him as a bulldog with a heart. Just before halftime he said to me, "Let's go—we're going to shake hands with Red Auerbach" (the legendary Celtic coach and general manager).

"You're kidding, right?"

"No," he responded. "I called his assistant and told her about our lifelong affection and pilgrimage to the Boston Garden." She had informed Red and arranged for us to shake his hand. As my brother led me right to Red's seat, I shook my head in amazement at what is possible if you just make up your mind.

How about you? What are the places, the experiences, and the people you'd like to encounter? Record your PEP goals here:

Places I would like to go:

1. _____
2. _____
3. _____

Experiences I would like to try:

1. _____
2. _____
3. _____

People I'd like to meet:

1. _____
2. _____
3. _____

Looking Back

Another powerful life lesson I learned from the work of Frankl was the impact of hypothetical retrospect. When a patient of his was struggling with an important decision that would have long-lasting consequences, he would invite that person to imagine him- or herself one year into the future, having already made the decision they were now contemplating. He described in *Man's Search for Meaning* that he would then ask them to answer the question, "Looking back now, one year after making this decision, *what do you wish you had done?*"

Quite often the person Frankl was questioning had changed her mind about what she would or would not do. I think this could be a profound exercise with a much larger mental leap forward. You've potentially got another 30-plus years ahead of you. Place yourself 30 years down the road: you are looking back on your accomplishments. What goals and objectives do you hope to have accomplished in these three decades that have now passed? Record your thoughts here:

For Myself: _____

For Others: _____

Enduring Attitudes

The attitude instrument in an airplane tells you how your wings are aligned with the horizon. When I ask people to define attitude, they often talk of a mood or feeling or perspective. Moods and perspectives are certainly impacted by our attitude but, fundamentally, attitude is nothing more than *choosing a direction and sticking to it.* If we enter any phase of life without keeping our eye on the attitude instrument, the winds of adversity will tilt us and we will lose our bearings—and more important, not make a safe landing. Attitude is the premier setting in our lives, as all other functions are eventually dictated by it.

I have always had a keen interest in the mindset and attitudes of those who thrive in later life and have sought out their life stories for the last 30 years. As a kid I read about Satchel Paige. Later, I read autobiographies of people like George Burns, Winston Churchill, Albert Schweitzer, and Linus Pauling. Being a writer, I especially loved the stories of Norman Vincent Peale, Studs Terkel, and Peter Drucker.

One salient characteristic that leaps from the biographies of the "enduring" is their ready wit and lively sense of humor, especially regarding themselves. That those exhibiting longevity seem to share *a self-deprecating approach to life* tells me that such an approach is crucial to reducing stress. The connection between stress and illness is well-established. The connection between one's attitude and stress level is obvious. Many of those I have read about seemed to possess not only a lively sense of humor but also other survivor attitudes toward life's stressors. Most were forward looking and concerned about the future as well as the present. Most refused to succumb to society's limiting views of age-related behavior and activity. They were people who truly believed they could control their own destiny. A MacArthur Foundation study on aging described how one ages successfully. The study used the phrase "a sense of mastery" to describe how individuals must believe in their ability to influence events and control their outcomes to be positive and productive in their later years. They found that during a period of less than three years, those who increased their sense of mastery also increased their productivity. The opposite also held true—those whose sense of personal mastery decreased saw a significant reduction in their involvement in productive activities.[5] What exactly is personal mastery? Self-reliance.

The person who takes a passive approach to life and lacks the ability to take action will experience a lack of productivity at any age. Typically, as people age, their belief in their abilities and their power to control their own destiny grows. However, this belief can, if allowed to do so, reach a point of diminishing returns. Experiments and experience have shown that if people are willing to try new things in their mature years, their self-reliance and effectiveness can flourish to all-time highs. Stories abound of people creating new boundaries in their lives in their later years—those who are flying on airplanes who have never flown, those who are taking up new courses of study, and those who are dabbling in new ventures and careers at ages others would consider old. Take, for example, Florence, who started driving an 18-wheeler semi at the age of 83—the oldest "rookie" in the history of the truck-driving industry!

As more of us prepare to spend a large part of our lives in "retirement," our attitudes toward this stage of life are extremely optimistic; 64 percent of us say we are currently enjoying either "the best" or "good" times of our lives. When you put a magnifying glass on the everyday activities and interests of these so-called retirees, you begin to see why they are flourishing and expressing enthusiasm and optimism. They are a dynamic and engaged group of people. They object to traditional labels given to their age group, such as *elderly*, *old*, or even *seniors*. They see themselves as experienced, wise, and seasoned. The numbers in these categories indicate a graying population that is healthy, active, adventurous, and more prosperous than ever before. These numbers only promise to rise with the influx of Baby Boomers in the 65-plus-year-old category between now and the year 2030. In the 1960s, there were 17 million Americans aged 65 and older. Today, there are approximately 37 million. By 2030 there will be 70 million aged 65 and older. That number will be somewhere between 20 and 25% of the entire population.[6] Depending on the attitudes you dictate for your own life, you can be one of the examples that your community will be talking about someday—someone who just gets better with age and rejoices with each day's opportunities.

You clearly have not reached the end of the road yet. There is a lot of territory to cover, and it might be wise before embarking on your next 100,000 miles to get "re-tired" ... some fresh tread will serve you well.

Money Is Only Part of the Equation: Investing Yourself, Then Your Money

Many people are so occupied with getting out of a career trap that they seem to care little about what happens after they leave their jobs. Despite the fact they have planned other aspects of their lives, they seem to feel retirement will take care of itself. The opposite is often true.

—Elwood Chapman and Marion Haynes,
Comfort Zones: Planning Your Future

As I travel around the world talking with audiences about the new approach to retirement thinking, I always start with the question, "When I say 'retirement planning' what's the first thing that comes to mind?" The universal answer is always "Money." This answer reminds me of the recently retired executive who told me, "I got the money piece together, what am I supposed to do now—hug my checkbook?"

The reason most of us think this way is because we've been taught to think this way. We've been inculcated for years that we needed to have a "number" that we would reach and then sail off into the sunset. In fact, one company's ad campaign even showed people carrying a giant number around the airport and other places. Those ads always irked me because they sent the wrong message. The quality of our lives cannot be guaranteed in a number. Instead of focusing on only a number we need to focus on a number of important questions:

- How will you spend the 168 hours that make up each week?
- How will you invest *yourself*, including your knowledge and wisdom, and experience?
- How will you invest your newfound freedom?

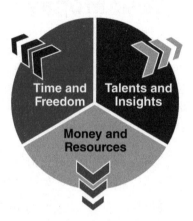

Don't fall for the logic that money is the only investment that matters in retirement. You've got three arenas of investment that require your attention and continual rebalancing:

- Time and freedom
- Talents and insights
- Money and resources

You have time and freedom to invest. Where will you focus your efforts? In this chapter, we'll go through some exercises to begin contemplating your liberation from a 9-to-5 (or longer) work schedule.

How will you invest your talents and insights? Are there philanthropic organizations out there that could benefit from your know-how and know-who? Perhaps there's a part-time gig out there for you to teach others what you have observed over a lifetime of use and practice. I've met many retirees who've gone down this path and are happier for it. You want to keep your "noggin joggin" or it could possibly wilt. This will be a theme we keep returning to throughout the book.

Then there's the money and resources piece to consider. How will your financial life change now that you're no longer cashing a paycheck? A woman I spoke with was a big giver in her community—she was having some angst about having to cut back on some of her contributions now that her husband had retired from medicine.

You'll also want to consider how you'll invest other resources besides money. Some people downsize, some earn some extra income by going the Airbnb route with either a primary or secondary home, others share with family and friends in order to spread the costs. It may take some creativity if your goal is to create more disposable income.

In all these investment arenas we need to consider our initial allocation, yearly review, and rebalancing as a part of the process. Remember, it's not a one-and-done proposition.

A Very Long Trip

A financial advisor who has been involved in financial planning for over 30 years told me this about lack of preparedness by people on the verge of retirement: "I ask the couple, 'What are you going to do in retirement?' And frequently I'm met with blank stares."

What difference will all our financial planning for the future make if we have no idea what kind of life we want to purchase with those financial resources?

Would you prepare for a two-week overseas vacation and not make any arrangements for how you will best use your time once you arrive? Only an intrepid adventurer or a cavalier fool would approach an expensive journey this way. Even just heading out for a short weekend trip can involve considerable time plotting out hotel, route, food, and entertainment options. Why, then, embark on a 30-year journey with the sole concern being economic? Millions are saving for what might be a journey of several decades—with absolutely no idea where that journey might take them. Individuals who approach retirement in this manner will have a ticket to ride but no roadmap (or GPS). While this may sound appealing, they may soon find themselves lost.

How important is it to you to have direction in the journey ahead? Existential preparation is more important than economic preparation if you plan on reaping enjoyment with your life moving forward.

Remember, money has no value in and of itself. Money is useful only in terms of what you can do with it. Just as important as saving for the future is having some sort of vision of what that future will be. Numbers crunching alone will not do the job. An inspiring vision of what you might be and do if you were financially able must accompany the numbers crunching if you hope to have a successful transition into whatever your next phase of life may be.

In 2008, when I was working on an earlier edition of this book, the National Endowment for Financial Education convened a think tank to discuss retirement planning. The think tank was not limited to financial professionals but included gerontologists, researchers, a social worker, and a psychologist as well. Some of the touchpoints that these varied professionals developed included:

- The picture of retirement has changed dramatically and will continue to change.
- Consumers have become more responsible for the success or failure of their own retirement.
- The financial services industry is realizing it needs to do a much better job of educating the public about the features, possibilities, and parameters of this new retirement.[1]

More than 10 years later, these touchpoints still matter. Although money is a primary concern in this new phase of life, it is just one of many. This report on the future of retirement planning stated, "Future retirees need to be asking what they want to do with their life during retirement, and what the personal implications of retirement are for them. Baby Boomers are looking for a meaningful role in their later adulthood. Money is important to them, but so is the quality of life in their retirement."

Where from Here?

One day Alice came to a fork in the road and saw a Cheshire cat in a tree. "Which road do I take?" she asked.

"Where do you want to go?" was his response.

"I don't know," Alice answered.

"Then," said the cat, "it doesn't matter."

—Lewis Carroll, *Alice in Wonderland*

Before you do the important work of crunching the numbers for the retirement stage of life, you'll want to crunch some numbers regarding life itself. I have prepared the *Retirement Life Profile*, a set of four tools for this purpose. In this profile, you have the opportunity to measure your approach to retirement life against the four philosophical pillars of the New Retirementality: Vision, Balance, Work, and Aging. In three of the pillars you will see a number that quantitatively expresses your progress toward a fulfilling life in retirement.

I developed these four pillars by identifying the most prevalent characteristics of successful (or failed) retirements:

1. *Vision.* Successful retirees retire *to* something; failed retirees retire *from* something.
2. *Balance.* Successful retirees find balance between vocation and vacation; failed retirees go from too much work to much leisure.

3. *Work.* Successful retirees keep themselves plugged into meaningful pursuits; failed retirees devolve into boredom and aimlessness.
4. *Aging.* Successful retirees focus on growing and well-being— what I describe as "successful aging"; failed retirees just take what comes.

By completing this profile, you will begin laying the foundation for a healthier stage of life. My hope is that if you do retire, you will do so on purpose—with purpose. Perhaps you'll never fully retire because the word retirement will be eradicated from your vocabulary. As George Eliot said, "It's never too late to be what you might have been." Let's get started.

Retirement Life Profile

Vision

> *I have come to the conclusion that more retirements will fail for nonfinancial reasons than for financial reasons.*
>
> —Michael Stein,
> *The Prosperous Retirement: Guide to the New Reality*

Don't think about retiring from something but instead to *something.* This thought has surfaced in my research as a hallmark of successful lives in retirement versus those that fail. Those who fail are thinking of retiring from something but have no clear vision of where they want to go—and end up being aimless. I've heard from scores of people who thought they wanted a life of complete ease but instead got a life of boredom. Creating a vision of what you want the rest of your life to look like is a critical part of developing your New Retirementality.

Sit down with your partner: each of you should select six pictures in the *Vision* exercise below and have a conversation around your personal vision of life. This exercise is simple and is intended to lead into a conversation with your spouse or partner, financial planner, life coach, or anyone else who may be helping you prepare for the next stage. Think about why you chose the images you did and how you plan on fulfilling those visions of life.

Visioning

Our *VISIONING PROCESS* in the *24 Things to do in Retirement* exercise will help you get a clearer picture of what you want to experience in the rich years ahead.

Directions: Choose 6 images (below) that fit your vision for retirement.

Travel	Explore	Play	Write
Relax	Teach	Go Back to School	Educate Yourself
Mentor Someone	Learn a New Skill	Develop a Hobby	Finish Unfinished Projects
Home Projects	More Time with Spouse	More Time with Family	More Time with Friends
Start a New Business	Continue on Present Course	Consult	Get Part-Time Job
Connect with a Cause	Volunteer	Get More Involved in Community	Take on a New Challenge

Balance

Did you know that every single person—from the billionaire to the person with few resources beyond Social Security—has the same amount to spend in retirement? As noted above, all of us have exactly 168 hours per week in their account. No matter how much money we have, if we do not have a plan for capitalizing on our time, we will not enjoy a fruitful stage of life.

Ever felt like life was just moving too fast? Ever felt like you just needed a little more time for your family or for yourself, to do absolutely nothing? I have found that many people who were workaholics their entire life find that they have forgotten how to enjoy themselves and live a life that balances work and play along with silence and activity.

We all need balance in our lives, whether we wake up each day thinking, "I can't believe I get paid to do this," or daydream about being a thousand miles away. While work may always be a part of our lives, we all need more. Taking time out to reconnect with our passions, enjoy a new experience, or spend time with family and friends is the yin to work's yang.

Living a balanced life leads to being a more balanced individual, which leads to being a pleasant person to be around. You may have to teach yourself how to live this way. The following exercise is a first step. Rather than jumping off the cliff of employment and hoping for a parachute to lead you to a safe landing, take a look at how you're spending your time now and what adjustments you would ultimately desire to make to order your life into a more tolerable pace.

Many people discover that a cold-turkey retirement is not the answer. They find themselves missing some of the activities and interactions and productive activities associated with work they did. What they really wanted was balance. Balance in work and play. Balance in family and personal time. Balance in running about and sitting still. Once this is achieved, life becomes quite exciting—but in a more quiet way.

In the worksheet below, do your best to analyze your current allocation of 168 hours a week, and then fill in your desired life portfolio and compare the two. Examine what areas are crying out for time in your life and figure out the changes necessary to make those adjustments happen. This way, you can get a visual representation of the life you have and the life you want.

NOW   DESIRED

Finding Balance

Finding balance begins by becoming aware of exactly how and where we spend our time. Each of us has exactly 168 hours each week to manage.

CURRENT LIFE PORTFOLIO

Directions: Determine approximately how and where you *currently* spend your time. (Total must be 168 hours.)

	Hours/Week	% of Time
• Family/Friends		
• Work/Career		
• Downtime (T.V., surfing the web, music)		
• Sleep		
• Health/Fitness		
• Personal Growth (hobbies, learning a new skill)		
TOTAL:		

DESIRED LIFE PORTFOLIO

Directions: Determine approximately how and where you *desire* to spend your time. (Total must be 168 hours.)

	Hours/Week	% of Time
• Family/Friends		
• Work/Career		
• Downtime (T.V., surfing the web, music)		
• Sleep		
• Health/Fitness		
• Personal Growth (hobbies, learning a new skill)		
TOTAL:		

What allocations can I make with my time to bring more balance to my life?

Work

What you spend your life doing should be fulfilling to you—period. If it's not, you need to take responsibility and commit to making a change. Life is too short to settle for a lukewarm existence. How do you go from collecting a paycheck to collecting a *playcheck?* If you're not spending your time doing something you find fulfilling, it's time for a career assessment and transformation. If you are looking toward retiring, you'll want to address the need for the expression of work, to some degree, in your life ahead. While most people don't conduct a work assessment before retiring, a high percentage end up taking on part-time work within the first year because they realize they were missing out on the positive aspects of work.

In this exercise, you have the opportunity to compare your working situation against the seven factors of fulfillment at work:

1. How well your talents and abilities are utilized.
2. Your enthusiasm level toward your work.
3. How much fulfillment you derive from the work you do.
4. The quality of the people you work with.
5. The growth you experience as a result of your work.
6. The benefit to others that is created through your work.
7. The degree that you are energized by what you do.

The last part of this exercise asks you to rank the work you do with the pay you receive. The worst possible ranking is a combination of hating your work and receiving terrible pay while the best possible ranking is absolutely loving your work and not believing you're actually getting paid what you are to do what you do. Most people fall somewhere in between.

With introspection, guidance, and persistence, you can find work that will reward you with a playcheck. The following exercise will help you determine how close you are right now. We'll talk more about the lifestyle benefits of work in the next chapter.

Collecting a Playcheck

Find work that unites your head, your heart, and your hands.

Directions: On a scale from 1 to 5, rate yourself on your true level of contentment, with 1 being "Not content" and 5 being "Completely content."

	1	2	3	4	5
1. I feel as though my natural talents and abilities are expressed through my work.	○	○	○	○	○
2. I have a continuing enthusiasm about the work I do.	○	○	○	○	○
3. I have a sense of serenity regarding my work.	○	○	○	○	○
4. I enjoy the people I work with.	○	○	○	○	○
5. I feel my work helps me to grow intellectually and personally.	○	○	○	○	○
6. I feel that I bring some benefit to others through my work.	○	○	○	○	○
7. I often feel energized by the work I do.	○	○	○	○	○

Directions: Read the 10 statements below and decide which one best describes how you currently feel about your job and pay. Then, click the corresponding number on the graphic below.

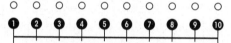

1. I dread my work and the pay is terrible.
2. I dread my work but the pay is decent.
3. I hate this work but the pay is excellent.
4. This work is okay but the pay isn't good.
5. This work is okay and the pay is okay as well.
6. This work is okay and the pay is excellent.
7. This work is great but the pay isn't.
8. This work is great and the pay is okay.
9. This work is great and the pay is excellent.
10. I'm having a blast and can't believe I get paid this kind of money to do it!

TOTAL [＿＿＿]

SCORING KEY

8–17   You are collecting a paycheck
18–24 Danger zone—change may be needed
25–35 You're on your way to a playcheck
36–45 Congratulations! You are collecting a "playcheck"!

Aging

The final cornerstone in preparing to succeed for the rest of your life is to shift from simply aging (getting old) to successful aging (what

I like to call "s-aging"). When I asked Mary, a 96-year-old dancer from a local dance studio, how she did it, she told me she just never stopped, but instead kept moving forward. I heard the same answer from a 70-something man shooting baskets at the local gym.

These people and others like them are examples of retirementors—they show us how to live with vitality and vigor for the rest of our lives. People stay young in mind, body, and spirit by staying active in mind, body, and spirit. Chapters 10 and 14 look at what some real-life retirementors are doing.

Successful aging is all about attitude. I'll bet you know someone who is 80 years old but acts like they are half their age, and vice versa, someone who is 40 and acts like they're 80. You're old when you think you are. S-aging is all about knowing what it takes to keep going—both mentally and physically—by challenging yourself every day of your life. Just because you're not 20 years old doesn't mean you can't be curious, challenged, connected, creative, and charitable. All it takes is the right mindset. S-aging is about thriving, not just surviving. In Chapter 15 you will find an in-depth discussion of the factors that lead people toward aging well.

What if we were as concerned and meticulous regarding investing our life energy as we are our financial assets? That is the biggest challenge ahead of you as you enter the phase known as retirement. No one retires for the purpose of decline or personal erosion. We want to plant ourselves in fields of fulfillment, however that may come to you. Your insights, your abilities, your passions, your interests, and your curiosities all matter and all need nourishing in the years ahead. Your spirit, mind, and body require attention and vigilance to steer clear of depreciation. The most important investment question facing you is, "How will I invest myself?"

C H A P T E R

The Retirement That Works

Just as iron rusts from disuse, even so does inaction spoil the intellect.

—Leonardo Da Vinci

In the Industrial Age, *work* became a four-letter word, saddled with the baggage of soulless tasks and exploitive industrialists. In the Modern Age, where the majority of us trade intellectual, relational, and experiential capital toward a paycheck, the very definition of work is going through a revival. We are squarely in a renaissance period in the evolution of what work means to our lives. In many ways we find ourselves in our work. We discover who we are and who we are not. We discover our strengths and weaknesses, but also at a deeper level we find affirmation of our purpose on this planet and of our potential to positively impact others.

In *Man's Search for Meaning* (Beacon Press, 2006), Viktor Frankl states that each of our lives resembles the work of a sculptor who chips away everything that is not, to reveal what is. Our work, in many respects, is a process of chipping away at the things that we are not, to discover who we are. We are literally hammering out our values to someday reveal the absolute best form that we can become. We can no longer afford to gloss over or ignore this core discussion for the next generation of "retirees" (for lack of a better term). We are in fact "searchers" or "remodelers" of our own lives more than anything else.

An irrefutable fact of our times is the potential collision at the junction of life where retirement intersects with our need and desire for work. I have had the privilege of participating in this meaningful discussion with thousands of retirees and contemplators of retirement through the publication of the four previous editions of this book and the hundreds of public presentations it has opened up to me. The discussion continues to expand in our culture and will no doubt become *the* key discussion regarding retirement in the decade ahead. A trend portending in this direction is the recent proliferation of "retirement coaches." As people seek to carve out a meaningful existence in the expanding middle-age years, they are seeking wisdom and direction regarding what specific role work will play in that existence.

Redefining Work

To help understand the role of work in the various stages of life, let's start with a broadened definition of work, and discuss the role work plays in our lives. Here's how I define work:

An engagement that brings value to others and meaning to me.

Note that this definition does not exclude work to compensatory activities. Volunteerism is included if the activity is valuable to others and meaningful to you. At the same time, "meaningful to me" should not be considered to be only activities where there is no compensation. I rejoice in the opportunity to engage in enterprises that bring value to others, meaning to me, not to mention a paycheck.

In his song "Real Life," John Mellencamp very nearly predicted the future reexamination of an aimless middle age and a workless retirement when he sang, "I want to live the real life, I want to live my life close to the bone. Just because I'm middle-aged, that don't mean I want to sit around my house and watch TV."

As we witness the great demographically driven expansion of the stage we call middle age, this is becoming an anthem of retirees. We clearly don't want to sit around and watch our midsections expand as our middle years extend. The trend of people choosing to work into their 60s, 70s, and even 80s is now a fact of life.

Whether people choose to work for economic reasons, existential reasons, or an amalgam of the two, it is indisputable that the trend toward working longer is part and parcel of the retirement discussion. Whether we want to or have to, we can no longer separate work from retirement—and that's good news for all of us.

Research from Rand points to the fact that people are choosing to work in retirement:

- 13.6% transition to part-time work
- 16.9% leave the workforce and subsequently reenter
- 25.7% remain in full- or part-time jobs past age 70[1]

According to the 2017/2018 Global Benefits Attitudes Survey, more than one third of all U.S. workers expect to retire at 70 or higher.[2] According to a Gallup poll, 74% of those polled planned to continue working either full or part-time, and a majority of those respondents were working because they chose to, not because they had to.[3]

The bottom line is that the retirement pitch for the last generation has headlined the benefits of leisure, but those who enter into it full time are finding that leisure alone cannot deliver the life satisfaction they seek. The exclusively leisure-life retirement is a mirage, a message I have been broadcasting for the past two decades. Individuals migrating from full-time contributors to full-time consumers cannot help but feel the existential shock to their systems. Self-indulgence is a poor prescription for a satisfying life. When some self-indulgence is balanced by service, relationship building, and exercise of aptitudes, it becomes a completely different story—with a much happier ending.

For good reason, over the past several years we've primarily been focused on the financial challenges surrounding retirement. What we hear far less about are the nonfinancial retirement challenges that people face:

- *Sense of identity loss.* You were Dr. Jones for 40 years. Who are you now?
- *Social/Relationship challenges.* What if you actually enjoyed the people you were working with or calling on?

- *Change/Reduction in mental stimulation.* Can sudoku really fill the bill?
- *Psychological issues around not getting a paycheck.* Inflation can quickly make you paranoid about going to a movie.
- *Extra time to fill in the day.* Are you wandering in the garage for something to break so you have something to fix?
- *Anxiety/Depression.* Your spouse doesn't seem too thrilled to have you around 24/7, does she (or he)?

These are the real, existential risks of retirement that we must wrestle with. Add to this list concerns about money, inflation, and uncertainty in the financial markets, and it is no wonder that more and more people are coming to the same conclusion—it works to work. And that doesn't necessarily mean full-time work, but enough to meet your emotional, social, and intellectual stimulation needs. The New Retirementality will be different for every individual. You may want to devote 10 hours a week to volunteerism, whereas someone else may never slow their 40- to 50-hour workweek until they completely expire—for the simple reason that their work energizes them. The critical conclusion that you should draw from this discussion is that work should always be a part of your life because it provides more than a paycheck.

Financial needs are only one piece in this puzzle when it comes to the New Retirementality. In the Gallup poll cited above, the percentage of "want to" work versus "will have to" work has edged up slightly since 2013. In addition, the percentage of respondents who wanted to keep working part time also rose—from 34% to 44%. The percentage of respondents who reported having to work dropped from 26% to 18%. From these findings we can conclude that people are choosing to continue working for more than just money—they understand the benefits of work to their health and well-being.

All the money in the world won't make a difference for those who feel they are losing their health, their connectivity, and their sharpness due to the lack of real challenge. Clearly, being challenged and active are now being mined not only for longevity purposes but for quality of existence as well.

Retirement is not a one-and-done decision, as all of us require time and experimentation to find the proper balance between vocation and vacation in our lives. One of the reasons for this is that as we mature, work can take on an entirely different meaning in our life. It can become about more than producing a paycheck and paying the bills. As we have already discussed, many people simply *need* to work—and not just for money. Let's take a look at some familiar stages of work and then discuss the destination many of us are aiming at and hoping for.

Longevity Works

In 2012, economist Josef Zweimuller at the University of Zurich coauthored a study that found that even though many crave early retirement, it seems to be bad for our health: "[A]mong blue-collar workers, we see that workers who retire earlier have higher mortality rates and these effects are pretty large."[4] The study showed that for every extra year of early retirement, workers lost about two months of life expectancy.

Two years earlier, in a 2010 article for CBS, Steve Vernon commented on the RP-2000 Mortality Study, which included a table that compared the annual death rates among two groups of men aged 50–70. The two groups consisted of men who were working, and then men who were fully retired. The death rates of those who were still working were roughly half those of men the same age who were fully retired. "What's going on here?" Vernon wrote, "I thought retirement was supposed to be good for you!"[5]

According to the *University of Michigan Health and Retirement Survey*, some of the potentially negative effects of retirement on physical and mental health appear to be related to lifestyle changes, such as declines in physical activity and social interaction. In other words, a working retirement is essential for both physical and mental health.[6]

Not everybody buys into the idea that working enables you to live longer and argue that longevity is linked to working engagements because people who are in poor health and disabled would fall into the retired group, and only healthy people can continue

no tiene lógica

to work. But their argument doesn't hold water, because those who were on disability benefits and in failing health were excluded from the studies that demonstrate longer life for those delaying retirement.

George Vaillant's book *Aging Well* (Little, Brown, 2003) summarized the correlation between a working engagement and longevity in detail (paid, volunteer, community engagement, or even hobbyist) as a primary factor in prolonging life. In the article mentioned above by Steve Vernon, he concluded that: ". . . finding powerful reasons for getting up in the morning in my retirement years is as important as my financial planning. We may need to work a little in our retirement years to make ends meet. In this case, I won't be bitter—working may be keeping me alive!"

Delaying retirement may stave off cognitive decline. A study of nearly half a million people by French researcher Carole Dufouil of the research agency INSERM found that for each additional year people worked, they reduced their risk of dementia by 3.2%.[7]

If you buy into these arguments, the caveat is that finding post-retirement opportunities or staying in the workforce as peers retire can be challenging for many—but not impossible.

According to psychologist Joann M. Montepare, "People can be as interested as they want to be, but if the positions aren't available, or if they don't have support through the transition, it can be difficult." Dr. Montepare serves on the board of the Boston-based group Discovering What's Next. The organization offers support and resources to mature workers who wish to embark on a second or post-retirement career and need guidance on figuring out what they want to do and how to retool their skills. The organization and others are attempting to increase awareness among local employers about how to appreciate, tap, and leverage older talent.[8]

Ready, Set, Engage

In one of its earlier surveys (2012), The Transamerica Center for Retirement Studies proposed the following definition of retirement readiness:

A state in which an individual is well prepared for retirement, should it happen as planned or unexpectedly, and can continue generating adequate income to cover living expenses throughout his/her lifetime through retirement savings and investments, employer pension benefits, government benefits, and/or continuing to work in some manner while allowing for leisure time to enjoy life.[9]

I find it interesting that work was included in their definition of retirement early on, and continues to be a part of "retirement readiness" in every survey since then.[10] Their definition reinforces the idea that "retirement" has now become an oxymoron—the latest generation to enter this phase of life that has made it so. Retirement is no longer a ledge of work we dive off while hoping our parachute is sufficient. Retirement is no longer an age marker where we have to hope shuffleboard and early-bird specials will fill our life expectations.

Modern retirees have no patience with stereotypes about aging—they are redefining retirement living. According to several studies, decisions are becoming more focused on social implications and intellectual stimulation, dispelling traditional myths that retirees are interested only in leisure activities. The new definition of retirement overwhelmingly advocated by today's retiree is one that emphasizes activity and engagement over leisure and rest. Retirement is a time to break out of the cocoon, not go into one. A minority of those in the traditional retirement age group preferred the definition offered by traditional retirement as "a time to take it easy, take care of yourself, enjoy leisure activities, and take a much-deserved rest from work and responsibilities."

It is important to note the diversity of the group embracing this new definition. It appeals to men and women, liberals and conservatives, all regions of the country, people in their 50s as well as those in their 70s, people who are limited by physical or medical conditions and those who are not. More than half of those in their 50s and 60s (59% and 52%, respectively) expect to continue to work into what would be previously considered traditional retirement years.[11]

Traditional retirement was premised only on wants, and society assumed that all retirees wanted were lives of leisure. The New Retirementality is premised on balancing needs with wants. Traditional retirement was focused on vacation, whereas the New Retirementality is focused on balancing vocation and vacation.

Retirement Planning That Works

Retirement is wonderful
If you have two essentials:
Much to live for, and
Much to live on.

—Anonymous

I have a very simple theory on the evolutionary role of work in our lives. What I mean by evolutionary is that our relationship toward work matures as we spend more time in the workplace. Clearly, we are not the same worker at 40 that we were at 25, and we are certainly not the same worker at 60 that we were at 40. Hopefully, as Frankl put it, we have chipped away large chunks of who we are not and are looking at a more vivid relief of who we really are as we enter our middle years.

Personal Missions

I am constantly on the lookout for people in mission mode because I'm keen on discovering what drives them. Flying home from a presentation in Florida, I began writing down thoughts about the place of work in our lives, specifically how we mature regarding our work. I came to the conclusion that there are four "modes" of work that we can pass through in our search for meaningful engagement:

1. We begin with the exploration mode early in life.
2. After taking on life responsibilities, many move into the utilitarian mode.
3. After a couple of decades, many migrate into the renaissance mode.
4. And some of us end up in the mission mode.

With the thought of *mission mode* in my head, I got up and walked to the galley area of the plane to see if I could get a soda. I began chatting with Frank, the lead attendant on the flight, asking him how the recent merger was going with the company's recently acquired airline. He responded by saying that there were definitely bumps in the road but that it didn't have a whole lot of effect on his working life because he "brought a certain attitude to work each day." He continued, "My work is my calling. It is my mission. I am here for you, the passenger, to make this the absolute best experience you can have. I am very blessed in my career. I see the world and get paid for it. I love seeing new places and all the perks that come with this career."

I told Frank that I was writing on that very topic at this moment and asked his permission to quote him. I was grateful for the instantaneous affirmation that we can evolve and mature through our work. We can eventually come to a place where our minds, our spirits, and our effusion of effort reach total assimilation.

One group at the leading edge of this discussion is Encore, founded by Mark Freedman of San Francisco. Check out their website, Encore.org, and you'll soon see how they promote the idea of combining purpose and passion for mature adults. They also have a program that helps organizations connect with mature workers. Their work is demonstrating that meaningful engagement is essential regardless of your age.

Mark Freedman makes the compelling case that the longevity revolution—pushing life expectancies closer to 100—is not adding to the end of our lives as much as it is adding to the "late middle" of our lives. Freedman says that a new stage of life is emerging—the working retired—as millions of Americans, who find themselves in a state of "suspended identity," are "un-retiring." Midlife is expanding like never before and work is a central theme in the discussion of this expansion. We can all benefit by answering the question, "What benefits of work mean the most to my well-being?"

C H A P T E R

Extending Your Stay by Staying on the Edge

Thus, one way to resist aging is to keep working; by doing this mature workers combat invisibility and "stay young" by "staying active."

— Sargent, Lee, Martin, and Zikic, 2013[1]

My friend Scott told me about a sad but instructive tour he was once given of a floor at his former company (a Fortune 100 company) in New York City. It was called the "Dinosaur Floor" and was literally a way station for employees in their late 50s and early 60s, who were, at best, static contributors but most likely were regarded as "hangers-on." Many of the residents were former big players in the organization, but for one reason or another were now regarded as irrelevant. They knew the reputation of their morose destination and also understood that the corporation was no longer looking at any of them as primary contributors. Nonetheless, they were abiding in a state of stalemate as the corporation was most likely attempting to avoid age discrimination lawsuits.

Scott's observation was that a lot of the people who ended up there had lost their relevance because they failed to keep up with key changes in the organization. They had plenty of experience and were battle-tested but had stopped learning. They had lost the pulse of critical knowledge regarding what was going on in the company and who the generators of change were. Like dinosaurs, they were respected because of the size of their footprint, but also like dinosaurs, they became extinct because they refused to adapt to their changing surroundings. Scott said it had nothing to do with their work ethic or even age. It simply had to do with being current and staying current. Scott told me he learned a valuable lesson that day: "The fact that you have 35 years in a company or industry means very little if you don't stay current—there is no badge for experience." Relevance is the key to survival.

My attorney, still practicing full time in his late 60s, said he observed a similar pattern among partners who had become irrelevant. The first thing he noticed was that they no longer read the trade journals, which is key for keeping up with the changes and trends in the industry. That was the first step in losing touch with the pulse. My attorney called it the beginning phase of intellectual laziness.

Staying in Your Zone

After speaking in New York City, I met Phil, who told me that he had retired from the Army at age 52—everyone's dream back in the 1990s. He knew he was much too young to "act retired," so he went to work for a year and a half at a major insurance company. His thought at the time was that working in customer service and reaping a reasonable income would be good for him. Phil soon discovered that the job was a long-term project that he wasn't really interested in sustaining after the Army. He wanted a game plan that energized him and knew he needed to get himself into a more energetic "zone."

Phil opted to go to a private company that engaged in transactional sales, which fit his personality very well. He ended up working there for eight years—full time. He then went on to work for the Commonwealth of Pennsylvania while continuing to work part-time at his sales job for another six years. I met Phil when he was 72 (he looked not a day over 60), and he is now working full time for the Commonwealth, enjoying the challenge and with no plans for exiting any time soon. I asked him if he had any advice for those who wish to extend their careers into their late 60s and 70s, and he offered the following observations:

1. Money matters. When I retired, my income dropped but my bills did not.
2. Sustainability matters. Trying to work at something that just "wasn't me" could not be sustained. Probably no job is perfect, but it has to be rewarding "enough."
3. Willingness to "bounce around" is a big advantage. It became obvious that knowing exactly what retirement would entail was not clear ahead of time—and I wasn't alone!
4. Older workers have a great "work ethic," which is apparent to employers who have used them before.
5. Older (retired) workers have a big "liability": if things get difficult, they can just quit. (I don't think employers know that yet, but I have experienced it as a supervisor!)
6. Younger workers have a lot to teach us.
7. Younger workers are quite interested in listening to and learning from older workers—if they (the older ones) respect them.
8. Being willing to take orders from a (competent) supervisor 40 years your junior better not be a problem.

Yes Sir, Kiddo

A 2014 Harris Interactive survey conducted on behalf of CareerBuilder found that 38% of American workers had a younger boss, up from 34% in 2012.[2] Aside from the implied challenges of reporting to someone the same age as your kid (or grandkid in some cases), there are communication preference challenges to overcome as well. Technology changes have a lot to do with this possible chasm in connecting. The younger generation's view is that "the dinosaurs" need to figure out how to get along with their younger and smarter superiors. You'll be expected to learn to communicate at their technological level and to respect their ways of approaching the job. It's either humble oneself and learn to adapt or off to the boneyard you go.

Claire Raines, coauthor of *Generations at Work: Managing the Clash of Veterans, Boomers, Xers, and Nexters in Your Workplace* (AMACOM, 2013), encourages the older worker to adapt to a younger boss's communication style rather than try to fight or change it.

Many mature workers can get easily agitated at the younger generation's mesmerized attention to electronic messages and avoidance of eye contact when communicating, but these days it's the norm, so you'll need to learn to deal with it.

A reader sent me an entertaining anecdote about an 87-year-old who taught a geography course at the University of Minnesota. He still utilized a 1970s-era slide projector in his class and refused to use a laptop. Being autonomous in one's profession affords one the luxury of resisting technology shifts, if desired, but the rest of the aging workforce will need to reset their attitude toward adapting and learning.

Jac Holzman is an example we would be better off emulating. Jac, a technophile from the start, started Electra records in his home in 1956; he eventually sold the company to Warner in 1970. In 2013, at the age of 81, having never lost his love of all things technology, he released an iPad app that chronicled the career of Jim Morrison and the Doors. When interviewed on why someone his age is dabbling in creating apps, Holzman quipped, "Wherever technology impacts music, I'm going to be there." We would do well to adapt a similar perspective on our particular field of interest and passion.

Raines advises that even when older workers make an effort to learn new modes of communication, they shouldn't expect reciprocity. You need to adopt your boss's habits. Don't expect him or her to learn yours. Robin Throckmorton, coauthor of *Bridging the Generation Gap: How to Get Radio Babies, Boomers, Gen Xers, and Gen Yers to Work Together and Achieve More* (Weiser, 2007), encourages older workers to take the initiative and have a conversation with their boss about the boss's favored mode of communication. Even 10-plus years later, that's still great advice.

The parties researching this phenomenon do agree that older workers shouldn't assume that having more experience will win them any degree of respect from a younger supervisor. "You have to earn that respect" is the advice of Throckmorton.

According to the U.S. Census Bureau, from 2025 to 2050, the older population is projected to almost double to 1.6 billion globally, whereas the total population will grow by just 34% over the same period.[3]

An article in "Diversity Insight" argues that it's important to include a mix of experience levels in workforce planning[4] while another report finds that there simply aren't enough younger workers to replace Boomers.[5]

As labor markets tighten, companies will soon have little choice but to welcome older employees. Smart businesses aren't waiting; they are already preparing to capture and encourage the contributions of older workers. Based purely on numbers (not enough workers to fill jobs), this approach will soon be regarded as a key competitive advantage. Most of today's businesses underestimate and are ill-prepared for how far this trend will expand. In an editorial in the *Harvard Business Review* in 2012, professors David Bloom and David Canning predicted the future: ". . . employees in significantly growing numbers will likely be able to work productively into their eighth or even ninth decade."[6] Not even 10 years later, we're seeing this come to fruition.

Bloom and Canning advise those who stay in the workforce to not expect their pay to automatically keep climbing all the way to the end of their careers. "Seniority-based pay sometimes exceeds performance at the latter stages of the life cycle," they write, but the effect will be that "bringing pay and performance (properly assessed) into closer conformity would likely ease corporate norms surrounding age at retirement." In other words, some younger workers may be getting more pay, but you're still getting the satisfaction of being employed and earning a paycheck.

Ageism on the Radar

According to an AARP Survey, "Nearly 2 out of 3 workers ages 45 and older have seen or experienced age discrimination on the job."[7]

Many of us will simply refuse to be categorized as unproductive simply because of age. There is a growing disdain among more mature workers regarding being shut off from mainstream workplaces. Often today, when a 60- or 70-something person hears terms like *senior citizen* or *golden-ager*, he hears them as euphemisms for "used up" or "useless." Today's employer will have to reassess hiring and retirement practices tainted with ageism. Gray hair and wrinkles are no reason to refuse admittance to or invite departure from a workforce if the gray matter is still intact and the desire is still present.

Societal and corporate laws and practices will have to change to accommodate updated definitions of *old* in our society. And have no doubt about it: the 60+ crowd will have the clout to get the job done. This is a generation that is defined by their abilities—not by their date of birth.

The Teaching Bridge

One method that many retirement-age workers are employing to keep their skills and minds sharp is to teach a course on their specific specialty in the marketplace or on a topic where they are experts. The design, development, and teaching of courses such as those offered at University of Wisconsin–Oshkosh are built on the model of older adults' creating learning opportunities for themselves and their peers within their local communities. These programs rely almost exclusively on volunteer instructors to develop and teach an array of classes for their members. The course offerings are extensive, and the course scheduling quite often copies the traditional college semester format of fall, winter, and spring terms. Is there a course you could teach for a local college that they could offer to your peers? It might be worth looking into local offerings in the learning-in-retirement space. What you may find is that some of your peers are doing the same and others are filling the seats. Teaching others will keep your senses sharp and your curiosity keen as you explore after-retirement opportunities.[8]

There is also a growing group of semiretired instructors in the Experience Corps (a part of AARP), which has more than 2,000 volunteers working at 20 inner-city schools and reaching out to more than 30,000 students who can really benefit from their experience, and spending time in classrooms, helping children achieve their potential. Volunteer Brenda Hall had this to say about her experience: "There was this one student who had some behavior issues. He wore a T-shirt one day that said, 'You are a genius.' And I said, 'What does your T-shirt say?' He didn't know. I said, 'Your T-shirt says, "You are a genius."' I said, 'Do you know what? You're a genius. You can do anything that other students can do. So, I want you to remember that when you put that T-shirt on, you hold your head high. You hold your head high and you say, 'I'm a genius.' From that moment on, I saw him grow to excellent on the behavior chart."[9]

If you want to stay sharp, stay engaged—even if there is no pay involved at the time. To be marketable one must be active, passionate, and involved with meeting needs on some plane. "Downtime" need not get you down if you raise your level of vision toward meeting needs that match up well with your competencies, interests, and drivers.

Advantages of Underemployment

A report from the Transamerica Center for Retirement Studies shows that most of us (56%) plan to continue working in retirement, including 14% who plan to work full time and 42% who plan to work part time. These findings are relatively unchanged since 2013 (54%). Though retirement historically has represented unemployment, you are better off being underemployed as opposed to unemployed. Aside from earning additional income, there can be access to employer health coverage and the opportunity to delay withdrawals from retirement accounts.[10]

The study reported that 62% of workers are taking care of their health so they can continue to work while slightly more than half (56%) are focusing on performing well in their current positions. Less than half (46%) reported they are keeping their job skills up to date, and just over 10% (13%) reported going back to school to learn a new skill. On a trip to speak in Florida, I was driven to my hotel by a Vietnamese immigrant who transported my imagination with his story of elasticity and resilience. He had been a "boat person," and his entire family escaped Vietnam in the 1970s on a boat so overcrowded that "if one person had leaned to the side, we would have all drowned—the water was up to the windows in the lower deck." It had cost his family their entire life savings to make the perilous voyage. He came to the United States in 1980, studied engineering, and went on to work for a major corporation for the next 30 years. Then they decided to downsize him. His options? Move to Germany and take work or stay in Florida and take bridge employment (in this case, driving a limo) and continue to look for work.

"I have a wife," he told me, "and she doesn't want to live in Germany. So I will do what I can until I can do what I want again. Family is more important to my life than the money right now."

If engineering work did not surface, he would begin thinking of starting his own business. I had no doubt that his positive, industrious, and resourceful attitude was the product of all he had lived through. This was just one more voyage—he had already survived the most dangerous one he would ever face.

The process of "recareering," as it is called in a study by Richard W. Johnson, Janette Kawachi, and Eric K. Lewis of the Urban Institute (*Older Workers on the Move: Recareering in Later Life*), is quite common and will become even more common if Baby Boomers— who are fast reaching retirement age—follow through on their plans to work in retirement. A large force of workers indicates that they want to try something new before fully retiring.[11] A study by the American Institute for Economic Research found the following:

- Most mature adults who are trying to change careers are successful.
- Most successful career changers report that the move has made them happier.
- Many successful career changers report that the change actually increased their income.
- Transferable skills are among the most important factors in successfully changing careers.[12]

EntreMature

Another interesting trend of our times is the number of traditionally retired-age individuals who are venturing into entrepreneurial pursuits. According to one study, more than half of the small business owners they surveyed (57%) were over the age of 50.[13] People over 55 are twice as likely to launch a high-growth startup as those under 35.[14] U.S. Census data reveal that the fastest growing new firms, including those in technology sectors or in entrepreneurial hubs, are founded by middle-aged and older entrepreneurs.[15]

Mature adults represent a growing share of new entrepreneurs, thanks to an aging population but also a rising rate of entrepreneurship among that group. I can be counted among this cohort, having launched two new enterprises in my late 50s.

In an article about entrepreneurship in older adults, Nancy Strojny, chairwoman of the Portland, Maine, chapter of SCORE, a nonprofit that offers free mentoring to aspiring business owners, states: "People should not buy the myth that all they need is a good idea. In reality, it's never the idea, it's always the execution."[16] The article went on to say that mature adults often have the unique skills required to start and succeed in business.

Helen Dennis, coauthor of *Project Renewment: The First Retirement Model for Career Women* (Scribner, 2008), says that the more seasoned veterans of work "know how to get information, connect with people, ask good questions. They come with experience and wisdom, know-how, and focus."

Finally, Andrea Coombes, author of the article referenced above, offers the following tips:

- *Take time to prepare.* Michele Markey says planning and research are the keys to succeeding. She is vice president with Kauffman FastTrac, a hands-on education program for entrepreneurs, sponsored by the Kauffman Foundation. "It doesn't guarantee success, but their chances of succeeding are greater." Her organization provides a self-assessment that shows how ready you are for the transition into entrepreneurship. This transition can't be taken lightly as the commitment of time and money can be quite significant. If you and your spouse are not on board, then transition may not go so well.
- *Get help.* Nancy Strojny of SCORE advises that you find someone who "will tell you the truth—not what you want to hear," said Strojny. People are "so in love with their idea" that they're often blind to the facts. SCORE offers mentors, but a former partner, peer, colleague, or long-time friend can also act as an advisor. You will want to consult with more than one person who has blazed the same trail to find out where the pitfalls are and what the price of commitment truly is to succeed.
- *Assess the investment required.* The most important question up front is, how much can you afford to lose? If you're going to tap your 401(k) and you don't have other reserves to fall

back on, it may be necessary to get a partner or not to pursue the venture at all. Experts advise that you resist the urge to lock in big costs up front, like renting a plush office space right out of the gate. "Until you really test the water that this idea has legs or traction, you don't want to tie yourself into fixed costs," Strojny said.

- Those who have succeeded often looked for shared work-spaces where they could rent a desk and office space. It is not only cheaper but can offer networking opportunities as well. "There are decisions that Boomers need to make that are unlike a 20-something," said Markey of the Kaufman Institute. Extra caution and prudence are required when the volume of earning years is behind you.

- *Consider a franchise.* "Franchising can be appealing to older entrepreneurs because the learning curve is shorter," Markey said. "A lot of the legwork has been completed. They're not having to reinvent the wheel," she said. The Entrepreneur's Source—which also happens to be a franchise business—offers free consultations to help people assess what type of franchise business might suit them. The company is paid a placement fee by the franchise if and when a person decides to buy in.

- *Bend but don't break.* After interviewing scores of people in their 60s and 70s who continue to sustain their place or continually reemerge in the workplace, the one thing I can point to as a contributor toward relevance in the workplace is elasticity. You may have to stretch yourself, learn new things, try out arenas that are unfamiliar, and deal with some neophobic emotions now and then. It may require a childlike curiosity at times and an aged resiliency at others.[17]

The stereotypically aging individual is the one who slowly but surely pulls in his or her periphery to be able to live within a rote bubble of repeated patterns and habits. The elastic persona and soul is just the opposite: constantly stretching, trying, examining, and experimenting to find what best suits him or her at this stage of life. This elasticity is attractive to others, motivating to you as an individual, and tends to push the periphery of possibilities outward instead of inward as you move further from your date of birth.

And always remember: to stay on the edge, you must never retreat from the edge.

C H A P T E R

Super-Septs: How 70 Became the New 50

We believe that it is time for aging measurements to account for the new reality of today's old age, including how well the elderly actually function.

—From an article in *The Conversation*[1]

I included the quote from *The Conversation* to start this chapter even though I've come to loathe our culture's glibness with the terms *old* and *elderly*. Even in the simple construct of our conversations, we can detect a pejorative tone with questions of age. Instead of asking, "How many years do you have?" (as the Latin languages do), we ask, "How *old* are you?" It's subtle, but you can see where it takes the conversation. We can and should be proud of the years we've gathered and survived. Nobody feels good about being viewed as old.

But as Bob Dylan sang, "The times, they are a-changin'."

People in their 70s and beyond are blowing past stereotypes and age-biased barriers with reckless abandon. They are rewriting what one can do when one doesn't let others tell them what they ought to be doing *at their age.* These so-called "older" people are healthier and achieving higher scores on cognitive status tests than they did in the past. People in their 80s are climbing mountains, running governments, and entertaining the masses. It's time to tell the truth on the matter: you're not old until you throw in the towel and claim your place on the park bench.

Feeling as Fact

How often have you heard someone say, "You're only as old as you feel," or "Age is just a number"? It turns out that these statements are more than a slight attitude adjustment for the sake of a more positive perspective. There is now scientific evidence that these statements (and the attitudes they convey) actually play a role in how well people maintain in good health or how quickly they decline.

The clichés about being as old as you feel are beginning to have real scientific backing. One study found that as people age, they continue to say they feel younger than their actual age.[2] The whole idea that we're supposed to feel badly about adding years is a distinctly modern bias that has its roots in the rise of retirement in our culture. It was at that point that, instead of prizing and venerating maturity, we started denigrating and relegating the "old" to the scrapheap. Now, with healthier approaches to life, we find ourselves surprised that we feel better than our age tells us we're supposed to.

I find this both amusing and ironic.

William Chopik, a professor of psychology at Michigan State University, conducted a study that surveyed over 500,000 Americans and found that as people got older, they nevertheless continued to feel younger than their chronological age.

> Sixty-year-olds felt like they were 46, Chopnik said. Seventy-year-olds felt like they were 53. Eighty-year-olds felt like they were 65. It looks like this is pretty consistent across age groups. People know that they are aging, but they are evaluating themselves and their lives and reporting feeling about 20 percent younger than their current age.[3]

This study surveyed people between the ages of 10 and 89 and found that views of age and aging change as we grow older. The more years you have, the more favorably you tend to view those years. Consistently, people in their 70s and 80s reported feeling younger than their years, yet teens and younger adults think 50 is old.

Chopik asserts that negative views about aging are communicated early in life through media, movies, and family views and attitudes: "These attitudes are present and pervasive already in childhood, so naturally it's hard to enact meaningful change to these attitudes—but that's what we're trying to do at the moment."[4]

Your View of You

Your attitude toward your age is the most important factor influencing your longevity, according to a study from the Yale School of Public Health.[5] The study, led by Dr. Becca Levy, found that those who acquired positive beliefs about old age from their surrounding culture are less likely to develop dementia—even if they carried a gene that put them at risk!

This was the first study to examine the idea of how culture-based views and beliefs on aging influence risk of developing dementia. The researchers studied a group of 4,765 people with the average age of 72:

> We found [that] those who expressed more-positive age beliefs at baseline were less likely to develop dementia . . . than those who expressed more-negative age beliefs," Levy said. She also added, "This makes a case for implementing a public health campaign against ageism, which is a source of negative age beliefs.[6]

So, it turns out that to remain healthy for longer periods, we need to insulate and inoculate ourselves from the age-negativity views and the crowds that disperse them. For many, that might mean spending less time with people your own age. Previous research[7] has revealed that for many, *age-group disassociation* may be just what the doctor orders.

If your everyday cohort has grown pessimistic, negative, cynical, and generally grumpy and malcontented, it's not going to help you maintain a positive view of your own status. Instead, be open to experience. The same research mentioned in the previous paragraph has shown that just being around negative age stereotypes can result in lowered self-esteem for mature adults. Some of the techniques they cited to help people distance themselves from these negative stereotypes included identifying with middle-aged adults and avoiding the curmudgeons out there.

Remember the story from Chapter 5, about the man whose father announced on his 70th birthday that he was going to start hanging around with younger people? That's what I'm talking about!

Do what you can to live to 100. It will be good for your kids. Your lifestyle and attitudes that carry you that far are contagious. A study examining the attitudes of the offspring of centenarians concluded that the centenarians' children have a stronger sense of purpose and meaning in their lives, compared with the general population.[8] Don't just leave them money—leave them with your wisdom!

Climbing New Mountains

In 1985, Richard Bass became the oldest person to climb all seven of the world's highest mountains. His ascent to the peak of Mt. Everest sealed his place in history. He was 55 years old.

Here's how things have changed. In 2013, Yichiro Miura of Japan reached the summit of Mt. Everest at the age of 80. By the way, it was his second time—he reached the summit in 2003 when he was 70.

Takao Arayama of Tanzania now holds the record formerly held by Bass of being the oldest to climb all seven of the highest peaks at the age of 74—he climbed the last of the seven mountains in 2010.

Over time, as life expectancy increases and people become healthier, mature people can and will do things that were previously the exclusive domain of the young. No one will be surprised when both these mountain-climbing records are broken, most likely within the next decade.

Take a look at our U.S. Senate. As of this writing, 5 senators are in their 80s, 18 are in their 70s, and 32 are in their 60s. The *median* age in our senate is 65 years, 199 days. Maturity has the majority!

In 2006, about 37 million Americans were 65 or older. By 2016, one of every seven Americans, or 49.2 million, had reached age 65. By 2060, that number will double: 98 million Americans will be at least 65.[9]

Simultaneous with the increases in the life expectancy and health of Americans, the labor force participation rates of 65- to 69-year-olds have jumped (according to figures from the U.S. Bureau of Labor Statistics) from 21.8% in 1990 to 32.2% in 2016.[10] This trend also promises to continue. They're not just there because they need to be. Many are there because they want to be.

Coaching Yourself Up

Within the next two years, Jim Boeheim will become the most mature coach in the history of Division I basketball. His current contract will take him through the 2022–2023 season, when he'll be

77 years of age. The previous record for longevity at this level was held by three coaches: John Chaney (Temple), Lute Olson (Iowa, Arizona) and Jim Phelan (Mount St. Mary's)—they all coached until they were 74 years old. Here's what Jim had to say: "I don't think we should put a number on how long you should coach or how old you should be. It should be illegal. Go as long as you can do a good job. It shouldn't be an age thing."[11]

I love that. He's right—it should be illegal. Think about it. John Wooden, the UCLA coaching legend, was forced to retire at the age of 65 due to California's mandatory retirement age for state employees. In Wooden's last year at UCLA, the Bruins won the 1975 NCAA championship.

I've seen retirement policies treat pilots, surgeons, professors, and CEOs the same way. It's ridiculous that we have any remnants remaining of such age-biased policies in any sector of our society.

Boeheim said he's a better coach now than he was when he was younger. He says most coaches actually do get better with experience.

"As you get older, you should be better at coaching," Boeheim said. "You learn your lessons. You keep thinking and learning about it, you should be better than you."[12]

Game Up

Another key that Boeheim cites is a workout regimen. If you've neglected this, it may not be too late to get started.

> I actually work out more now than I used to. I didn't work out from 30 to 68. I just started working out when I turned 68. I wouldn't be physically able to coach if I didn't start doing (Pilates) four years ago. I needed to do Pilates to get my core stronger. It's done that. If my knees weren't bad, I'd be perfect.[13]

A Ball State study on Cardiovascular and Skeletal Muscle Health with Lifelong Exercise analyzed septuagenarians who have been exercising for decades. The study, led by Scott Trappe, found that these septuagenarians have heart and lung capacities and muscle fitness like healthy people in their early forties.[14]

For the average study participant—characterized as a lifelong exerciser—working out was a hobby. On average, each exercised about five days a week for about seven hours total. Trappe and his 11-person research team said the benefits of the study should be obvious for the average person: 30 to 60 minutes of exercise a day may be *the* key to a healthy life. ~~5 day a week~~

Cardiovascular health was gauged by having participants cycle on an indoor bike to determine VO_2 max, which measures the maximum amount of oxygen a person can use during intense exercise and establishes aerobic endurance. Each participant also had a muscle biopsy to determine how capillaries formed and aerobic enzyme activity. Our VO_2 max normally declines by about 10% per decade after age 30.

The age-related reduction in VO_2 max is directly associated with an increasing risk of multiple chronic diseases, mortality, and loss of independence. The septuagenarians were found to have slowed this decline by their cardio-regimens, prolonging healthier years ahead. Get on your bike and pedal like your life is on the line—to some degree it is. Of course, if you're approaching or past 70, I'm just preaching to the choir. According to a recent survey in the UK, *Super-Septs* go to the gym more than any other age group.[15]

The *Daily Telegraph* reported a Nuffield Health survey (with 75 gyms in England and Scotland) that showed that 72-year-olds went most often, with an average of eight visits a month, while those aged 70 to 79 went 7.5 times a month. Compare this to the 20 to 25 age group, who go 6.5 times, and the 25- to 39-year-olds, who go to the gym six times.

I'm sure you've seen this trend at your gym. At my gym, I see many people in their 70s, 80s, and beyond working out on a daily basis. For some, working out just means showing up at the gym, but I'm glad that they're there nonetheless.

Voices of Encouragement

As you've probably surmised by now, I'm a sports fan. Having been raised by a sports journalist, it's in my DNA. I was raised to appreciate and venerate the talent behind the microphones, listening to radio legends such as Harry Carey and Jack Buck.

Today, I can't help but notice the impact of septuagenarians and octogenarians in the broadcast field as well. As of this writing (2019) basketball analyst Dick Vitale is 80 (with the enthusiasm of an 8-year-old); Marv Albert is 77; Bill Rafferty is 75; NBA analyst Hubie Brown is 86! Hubie is as sharp and incisive today as he was 30 years ago. The legendary Dodger broadcaster Vin Scully made his iconic baseball calls into his 89th year. Every time I hear one of these voices on the radio or television, I'm inspired and encouraged about the future of maturity.

Turning the Corner

It's time to dump the talk about being "over the hill" and instead focus on talking about eliminating ageist stereotypes. According to the Reframing Aging Initiative, people may hope for good health and happiness, but they still tend to believe that growing old is all about deterioration and decline.[16] The fact remains that aging produces some degree of decline, but we *can* slow the progression and put off into the future a large degree of both physical and mental decline.

There's a Bible verse that says, "Though outwardly we are wasting, yet inwardly we are being renewed day by day" (2 Cor. 4:16, NIV). There is a definite relationship between the inward and the outward. I don't jump nearly as high as I once could on the basketball court. I'm not as fast or quick, either. But this doesn't stop me from going and competing against the kids. In fact, I think it inspires them to periodically get whupped by the "old guy." My dad is approaching 85 and still goes to the outdoor court to shoot baskets a couple of times a week. That inspires me.

We can do something about the ageist prejudices and perspectives in our society. Patricia Devine, a professor of psychology at the University of Wisconsin–Madison, studies ways to reduce prejudice. According to Dr. Devine, we need to "tune in" to our individual "habits of mind" that usually go unexamined.[17]

But Devine says resolve to change these habits falls short. We need strategies to turn the corner on any form of prejudice. The strategies she recommends include:

- *Replace stereotypes.* This entails *becoming aware of and then altering responses* informed by stereotypes. For example, instead of assuming a senior with a cane needs your help, you might instead ask, "Would you like assistance?" This question shows that you respect the other person's autonomy.
- *Embrace new images.* This involves thinking about people who don't fit the stereotype you've acknowledged. This could be a group of people (older athletes), a famous person (TV producer Norman Lear, who, at 95, sold a show on aging to NBC), or someone you know (a cherished older friend).
- *Individualize it.* The more we know about people, the less we're likely to think of them as a group characterized by stereotypes. Delve into specifics. What unique challenges does a mature person face? How does that person cope day-to-day?
- *Switch perspectives.* This involves imagining yourself as a member of the group you've been stereotyping. For example, how would you feel if strangers patronized you and called you "sweetie" or "dear"?
- *Make contact.* Interact with the people you've been stereotyping. Visit and talk with that friend who's now living in a retirement community.

A New Season

We have not witnessed great strides in life expectancy in our generation but with *life quality* at later stages of life. Today, a septuagenarian with the right attitude and regimen is still in the prime of his or life.

We have plenty of great role models around us and in our culture to remind us that our internal resources can be regenerated and sparked as long as we choose. Let's adjust our attitudes and approaches accordingly for one simple reason: it's the most important antiaging move we can make. The research is in and the conclusion is clear—age really *is* just a number!

Redefining *You*: What's Your Retirementality?

Life is a delicate balancing act: between vacation and vocation,
between connecting with others and doing something for yourself.
—Mitch Anthony

When you buy a new set of tires, most tire shops will tell you that they will rebalance those tires at no charge to help you get the optimum life from your purchase. How often do you take advantage of the offer? If you're like me, you probably tell yourself that you will stop in periodically to check the balance, but actually you don't reappear until one or more tires has been worn down or you're experiencing a wobbly ride, and you are now forced to make another purchase. The analogy here is that simply by virtue of use, things tend to go out of balance—and so it is with our lives.

We're focused on our journeys and busy with our busyness. We begin to notice that the ride doesn't seem as stable or smooth as it once did, and we find that we are again out of balance. We're working too much. We're not seeing the people we want to see. We're not enjoying the activities that restore and invigorate us. We don't have any time to sit still and reflect. The balancing act of life is a dynamic challenge requiring a dynamic solution (continual reassessment). There is no such thing as a one-and-done rebalance for our lives. The tread gets worn and our alignment shifts by virtue of motion.

Achieving balance in life is a matter of constant focus and vigilance. Any good thing taken beyond the bounds of balance is no longer a good thing. Life is full of illustrations, as seen in the following about stepping over the invisible lines of imbalance:

- Physical rest becomes laziness.
- Physical pleasure becomes licentiousness.
- Enjoyment of food becomes gluttony.
- Self-care becomes selfishness.
- Self-respect becomes conceit.
- Cautiousness becomes anxiety.
- Being positive becomes insensitive.
- Loving kindness becomes overprotection.
- Judgment becomes criticism.
- Conscientiousness becomes perfectionism.
- Quietness becomes noncommunication.
- The enjoyment of life becomes intemperance.
- Interest in possessions of others becomes covetousness.
- Ability to profit becomes avarice and greed.
- Generosity becomes wastefulness.

There is an invisible line that we come to and can cross in all areas of life that marks the difference between balance and imbalance, discipline and mastery, and chaos and control. We must constantly address and regulate the individual compartments of our lives to keep any particular focus from spinning out of control. Once we identify where the lines are that we should not cross and then develop emotional and logical thought patterns to keep us from crossing those lines, we can achieve what is commonly called maturity.

New Spin on Re-tiring

Now we come to the specific balance desired in the retirement proposition. We have already established that a life of total ease will not satisfy. Neither will a life of "nose to the grindstone" without any respite. But the challenge, especially as couples retire, is that balance is a highly idiosyncratic proposition. What constitutes balance to you may be perceived as boredom to someone else.

What constitutes balance to one person may be perceived as "too much going on" to that person's partner in retirement. How we each define retirement is as unique as our fingerprints.

For years, observers, researchers, and authors have been trying to reframe the retirement discussion by changing the term from *retirement* to something else. The word *retire* means "to withdraw," and the Baby Boom generation's discomfort with the notion of withdrawal has fueled the discussion for well over a decade. I've read about *re-firement, re-hirement, re-wirement,* and a slew of replacement terms, like *renewal, renaissance,* and more. These efforts have been in vain as the term *retirement* is firmly entrenched in the life-course lexicon of modern life, in spite of its morphing meaning and definition.

So, given this nomenclatural fact of life, I'd like to share an idea that my friend and sometimes coauthor Scott West proposes: keep the term *retirement* but alter its meaning. Since retirement is no longer considered an ending point on the map but more of a launching point, instead of withdrawing we intend to *recalibrate.* What we need before we embark on our journey is to "re-tire" our vehicle—we need new tread for the journey ahead. Instead of hitting the final rest stop of life, we are now looking ahead to our next 100,000 miles. To re-tire, then, is to prepare for the altered state of life ahead of us.

Thanks, Scott, for the idea. Now let's get busy getting re-tired. The analogy seems to jibe with the concept of balance and the fact that, as people embark upon retirement lifestyles, there are four primary categories of focus (the four tires if you will): *Vacation, Vocation, Renewal,* and *Relationships.* The task ahead of you is to idiosyncratically design a plan for balance that suits your temperament, your goals, and your specific situation.

I recently gave the profile in Figure 11.1 (My Retirementality™ Profile) to a retired couple in which the husband had been in the retirement phase much longer than his wife, and they were struggling with how to manage their new schedule together. She didn't have any desire for more work but found herself becoming restless within a few months' time. He has worked three hours every day for the duration of his retirement years. After filling out the profile, many of their questions and the root of their recent discomfort became apparent—they realized, as individuals, they had unique personalities and perspectives toward retirement living.

My Retirementality™ Profile

Directions: *Within each group, choose the phrase that best describes you, with 4 being the most accurate and 1 being the least accurate. Total each letter on the bottom of the page. Do not leave any spaces blank, and be sure each group has a 1, 2, 3 and 4 rating.*

SAMPLE

A **3**
B **1**
C **4**
D **2**

A___I love to kick back and relax.
B___I love to spend time with family and friends.
C___I love exercising.
D___I love my work.

A___I want to play every day.
B___I want to plan some family trips.
C___I want to pay more attention to my well-being.
D___I want to use my abilities to help others.

A___I want to spend more time on hobbies and other interests.
B___I want time to travel.
C___I want to exercise more.
D___I want to continue to do the work I do.

A___I want to start working on my "bucket list."
B___I want to start making memories.
C___I want to focus on being in top shape.
D___I want to make a difference in the world.

A___I want to get away from work.
B___I want to spend more time with my spouse.
C___I want to expand my interests.
D___I want to continue doing what I do for the rest of my life.

A___I want to wake up to an empty agenda.
B___I want to be more involved in the community.
C___I want to increase my energy level.
D___I want to feel challenged on a daily basis.

A___I want to visit a lot of places.
B___I want to catch up with a lot of friends.
C___I want to make staying healthy a priority.
D___I want to continue competing and finding new challenges.

A___I have many interests that take up my time.
B___I look forward to spending time with friends.
C___I want to lower my stress level.
D___I want to continue being able to use my skills.

A___I look forward to "every day is Saturday."
B___I look forward to spending more time with the people who are important to me.
C___I look forward to more personal growth.
D___I look forward to interacting with people I work with.

A___Free time is my top priority.
B___I want to invest in relationships.
C___I want to find some balance.
D___I am completely engaged in what I do professionally.

Add up totals for each and record in the box below.

TOTALS: **A =** ☐   **B =** ☐   **C =** ☐   **D =** ☐

Figure 11.1   My Retirementality™ Profile

My Retirementality™ Profile

Directions: Once you've totaled your findings, graph your "A" total in the Play column, "B" total in the Connect column, "C" total in the Renew column, and "D" total in the Work column. Draw a line to connect the dots. The results will help you and your advisor determine what is important to you and how to integrate your profile into your plans for the future.

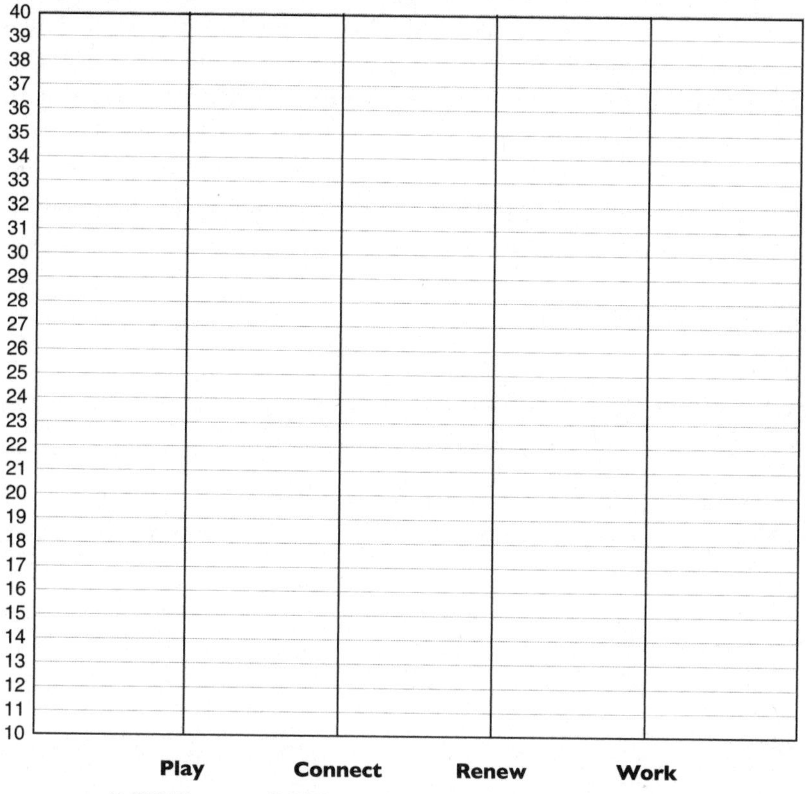

	Play	Connect	Renew	Work
40				
39				
38				
37				
36				
35				
34				
33				
32				
31				
30				
29				
28				
27				
26				
25				
24				
23				
22				
21				
20				
19				
18				
17				
16				
15				
14				
13				
12				
11				
10				

Play (A TOTAL)_____ **Connect** (B TOTAL)_____ **Renew** (C TOTAL)_____ **Work** (D TOTAL)_____

LEGEND

A. PLAY = LEISURE, TRAVEL, HOBBIES

B. CONNECT = TIME FOR FAMILY/FRIENDS

C. RENEW = PHYSICAL/MENTAL WELL-BEING

D. WORK = PROFESSION, HELPING OTHERS

Figure 11.1   (Continued)

Play

If you look at the simple chart in Figure 11.2 (My Ideal Week in Retirement) and first fill in your play activities, including leisure time, hobbies you'd like to engage in, and travel you'd like to pursue, you might reach some quick realizations regarding available time and your use of it. Usually, when I encounter people whose retirement dream is to "have nothing to do but play golf," I ask them to fill in their tee times. They enthusiastically block out the morning spaces on all seven days or sometimes five days. They now have 70% of their time staring back at them as whitespace. Suddenly, they realize they have made zero preparation toward activities to fill those blocks of time.

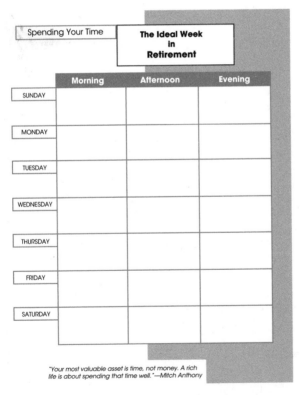

Figure 11.2   My Ideal Week in Retirement

A weekly calendar will not represent all the ventures and engagements of an entire year, but it will give you a pretty good clue concerning the cadence of life you are directed toward. You probably won't be going on a trip every week, but you most likely will engage in hobbies and leisure several times in a seven-day period. Go ahead and fill in your calendar with work, play, connecting, and renewing activities by asking yourself, "What is the best use of my time during each day?"

Work

Keep in mind that work is no longer an either/or proposition when it comes to retirement; it is more of a *how much* proposition. How much do you need or want to work? How much do you enjoy the engagements that work brings to your life? Gauging your capacity for work in your 60s to 90s is a highly idiosyncratic exercise— no other human can answer for you or know what work does or does not mean to you as an individual. The correct balance of work for you is determined by a number of factors including, but not limited to:

- How easily you are bored.
- How much you like your work.
- The potential strain on a marriage as the result of your being home all the time.
- Your need for additional income.
- Your energy level.
- The importance of your social network at work.
- Your need for competition.
- Your need for relevance.
- Your level of motivation and drive.
- Your need to create and make an impact.

The other factor to keep in mind while analyzing your retirement personality is that all of these factors (work, play, connect, and renew) are dynamic in nature and can fluctuate from year to year, depending on the circumstances you face. You may be heavily inclined toward play or work, but if an unforeseen event like illness or injury takes place, your focus may steer toward connecting and personal renewal and then revert back again to your original focus once that particular period has passed.

Our lives are as unpredictable as are our responses toward circumstances we have yet to face or navigate through. Think of this profile as a measure of your DNA regarding the retirement lifestyle and as a compass for how you will navigate in the years ahead. No decision is permanent as long as there is potential for unexpected opportunities and temporary setbacks.

Connect

How much time you spend in connecting activities will vary with the geographical spacing of you and those you hope to connect with. If your children and grandchildren are in close proximity, then your schedule will most likely reflect that focus in your retirement profile. If your grandchildren are 3,000 miles (and a full day of travel) away like mine are, then the connecting calendar will be more annual, semiannual, or holiday driven. One chief consideration for those who place a high premium on connecting with others in their retirement vision is: *How much connecting does the other party seek?*

I'll never forget the scene in the movie, *About Schmidt,* where Schmidt, a retired insurance underwriter played by Jack Nicholson, is forced to face his illusions about connecting with his daughter in a neighboring state. He held the idea dear and set out from Omaha to Denver in his RV to see her. The scene occurs a couple of days into his long-imagined visit, when he is sitting in a hot tub with a woman (Kathy Bates) and his daughter, and she asks him how long he plans to stay around. The disinviting tone is impossible to miss. The next morning he turns his RV back toward Omaha.

On a more inspiring note, I was once approached after a speech in Minneapolis by a woman who told me how making a weekly connection with her little girl had made a profound impact on her newly retired father. Six months into his retirement, the family began having concerns and encouraged him to get checked out at the clinic. The diagnosis revealed the initial signs of cognitive impairment, indicating the development of dementia. Everyone in the family had noted the aimlessness that had marked his days since retirement. His daughter, sensing his need for purposeful engagement, asked him if he would be willing to watch her daughter one day a week (the signs weren't significant yet to warrant fear); he enthusiastically agreed. At the time of my talk, this arrangement had been going on for over a year. With misty eyes, his daughter told me that he had recently been to the doctor and all signs of the developing dementia had disappeared. Sometimes an ongoing connection can be a life saver.

Renew

The quest for renewal takes on many unique and individualized forms for every person. For some, it is attending to a hobby that brings them serenity and fulfillment, such as gardening.

For others, renewal means attending to personal growth in areas where they feel a sense of neglect. These can range from taking self-improvement courses, to obtaining new degrees from a university, to embarking on a spiritual pilgrimage, to creating a radical change in one's pace and "trying on" a new way of living.

For some people, a period of renewal simply means not working. For these individuals, being free from vocational obligations, schedules, and commutes is the source of their renewing. After a time of chilling, I've seen many of these temporary retirees gain a sense of clarity, centering on what they want to do next. For some, it is a cause they want to engage in, while for others, it is an almost forgotten goal or pursuit they are ready to dust off and make a run at with their newfound energy.

The retirement era focus on renewal is driven by a need for balance, meaning, and peace of mind that many have found lacking in their vocational pursuits and schedules. Some feel they have lost touch with friends and family, some have forgotten how to play, some feel they have lost touch with balanced living and relaxation, and some are feeling the dearth of time to attend to their own interests and inclinations. A major driver in this period of life is about aging well.

In an article titled "Reinventing Retirement: New Pathways, New Meanings," the authors say that for some, one way to resist aging is to keep working; by doing so, mature workers combat invisibility and stay young by staying active. Others reported defying age through active self-work and disciplining the body through exercise and keeping fit.[1]

A whole generation of retirees is learning to resist aging by keeping active and fit. Go to your local health club or gym and note the average age of the participants. According to Meredith Poppler, vice president of industry growth at the International Health, Racquet and Sportsclub Association, the group age 55 and older has grown more than 500% since 1990. The second-fastest-growing group for gym memberships, people under 18, pales in comparison (less than half that number).[2] Renewal is an important topic for many new retirees as they are hoping to discover how to stay younger due to an increase in their subjective well-being. They are feeding their human needs, thus causing a spillover effect onto other domains in life. In *Quality of Life Therapy* (John Wiley & Sons, 2005), Michael B. Frisch defined 16 areas of life to elevate our well-being. They are in the list that follows. How would you rate your current state in regard to these 16 areas?

Health	1	2	3	4	5
Self-esteem	1	2	3	4	5
Goals/values	1	2	3	4	5
Money	1	2	3	4	5
Work	1	2	3	4	5
Play	1	2	3	4	5
Learning	1	2	3	4	5
Creativity	1	2	3	4	5
Helping	1	2	3	4	5
Love	1	2	3	4	5
Friends	1	2	3	4	5
Children	1	2	3	4	5
Relatives	1	2	3	4	5
Home	1	2	3	4	5
Neighbors	1	2	3	4	5
Community	1	2	3	4	5

As I look at this list, it is clear that the majority of these items are pretty important to most human beings. The one element that does not elevate to the level of the others in terms of importance in our modern times might be _neighbors,_ as it depends on the type of neighborhood or area you live in. If you are in an area with great swaths of space between you and your neighbors, there is a good chance that being neighborly wasn't a great motivation for moving into the neighborhood. But the rest of the list contains elements that most of us will acknowledge have a bearing to varying degrees on our well-being—underscoring the idea that life, at all times, is a great balancing act.

CHAPTER

Redefining Rich: Bridging the Gap between Means and Meaning

To allow me to do what I want to do every day.
—Warren Buffett on the meaning of money

Legend has it that Harry Houdini, the famous escape artist, walked into a jail cell—the door clanged shut behind him. He worked for two hours, unable to make his escape. Completely drained from the experience, Houdini collapsed in frustration and failure and fell against the door. To his surprise, the door swung open—it had never been locked. The door was locked only in the mind of Houdini.

Whether the story is legend or fact, we would all do well to consider what needs to happen to bring a greater sense of meaning to the means we gather in our working lives, and free us from feelings of futility, frustration, insignificance, and even failure. Once that door is opened, everything else, including our material management, can be ordered in such a way as to accelerate and accommodate a more meaningful existence.

In this chapter, we are going to reframe the conversation around building wealth toward *living rich*, as opposed to simply *getting* rich. One is a state of contentment and purposeful being while the other is a discontented chase that never ends because there simply is no exit ramp. A friend of mine who works with ultra-wealthy people in a major metro area conducted a survey that asked, "How much money would you need to have to consider yourself rich?" Those with $25 million said the number was $50 million. Those with $50 million said the number was $100 million. Those with $100 million said the number was $200 million. The first group who would admit that they were already rich were those with $200 million.

In many respects, you could take the preceding illustration and plug in the numbers you want ($250,000 to $500,000 to $1 million, or $1 million to $2 million to $3 million), and you will get the same existential conclusion: discontentment is hardwired into the culture and attitude of the majority. If you can find contentment wherever you are, you already are "richer" than those who have the means but lack the attitude to enjoy what they have gathered. Our perceptions around what money can and can't do for us have a great bearing here, as does facing the reality that more money can also mean more stress and more responsibility.

A survey by Schwab found that wealth meant "having a lot of money," followed closely by "enjoying life's experiences," "being able to afford anything they want," and "living stress-free and having peace of mind." Survey respondents, on average, reported that you needed $2.4 million to be considered wealthy, but they also mentioned things money can't buy: having good physical health, gratitude, and building community.[1]

We live in a world that is obsessed with increasing ROI (return on investment) when we should be more concerned with achieving ROL (return on life). "Return on life" is a phrase I developed to define the ultimate purpose of gathering and investing materially. No one gathers only for the sake of gathering. Even the greedy and acrimonious have an extra-material purpose for gathering, whether it is conceit, power, or extreme insecurity.

The first question that should be asked and answered in a money management conversation is not "What kind of return are you hoping for?" but rather "What is the money for?" The end objective should inform all decisions that are made around the management of your means. Meaning leads the wagon instead of following it. We don't live purposefully by expending everything we have toward gathering the most money possible—and just hoping that something meaningful happens on the way. We live purposefully by *investing on purpose*—deciding up front why we want the money, and deploying those means in a fashion that fuels meaningful pursuits.

Another perspective we hear too little of is that the focus on building wealth is not without consequence. A study by U.S. Trust on Wealth and Worth asked the following question: "What would make life better?" Almost half (46%) responded with "more time," and more than half (58%) responded with "more connections with family and friends." Interestingly, less than 20% (19%) cited "more money." Sixty percent agreed that the demands on their time have increased as their wealth has increased, and 51% agreed they were also dealing with more complicated issues and decisions. If someone happened to own a business, they were even more likely to feel being under pressure (72%). Clearly, we need to count the cost of chasing bigger numbers. For some, the bottom line is that they can ill afford the wealth they seek.[2]

> *Money is a terrible master. If it gets over you and you get under it, you become its slave.*
> —E. Stanley Jones, theologian

In the course of asking people what gives meaning to their lives, I often hear answers that include happiness, fulfillment, balance, satisfaction, security, significance, and success. When people use these words, their answers reveal unique elements to a meaningful life that add a great degree of clarity to their lives. Success is not the same as significance. People can be enormously successful by monetary and other standards and feel that what they do is not significant. Happiness can easily be differentiated from security, and it is possible to have one without the other.

As we look forward to a meaningful transition in our lives, we need to understand how intangible elements can, together, define a meaningful and contented life. A meaningful life is a life full of meaning. The conversation around money matters should not exclude meaning, but rather meaning should be placed at the very center of the conversation: *How can I get the most meaning from my means?*

There are many aspects of our lives that give us a sense of fulfillment—family, achievement, exploration, freedom, and altruism are some of them. For the sake of clarity, I am going to define these as "the seven meaningful intangibles." Many times, people can have a personal epiphany when they understand these goals for what they are and stop looking for them in the wrong places.

The Seven Meaningful Intangibles

No trumpets sound when the important decisions of our life are made. Destiny is made known silently.

—Agnes de Mille

Happiness Is Wanting What You Already Have

This is not the Madison Avenue definition of happiness. In fact, this definition is the polar opposite of the advertising industry's mantra that "happiness is having more than you have now." This old and worn sermon is one we have heard a million times: things won't make us happy. Yet we watch the ads and accept the underlying message that possessions define us. Shortly after the invention of the coin in ancient times, the Greeks came up with the phrase *oremata aner*, which means "money is the man." It didn't take long after the invention of what we call *money* for it to become a metaphor for much more than the ore it was composed from. It soon became the measure of a man's abilities, his value, his skill, and ultimately his worth. Has this changed over the centuries? Hardly.

If anything, the message has only been further imprinted into the soul of mankind, ultimately establishing money as the religion that rules secular existence. We begin to develop a keen sense of peripheral vision regarding our neighbors' homes and the possessions filling those homes. Soon, we, too, have assumed the definition of happiness that Madison Avenue has designed for us. *Oremata aner* is the mantra of Madison Avenue's efforts.

But the true key to happiness is not in getting those things; it is in changing what you want. If you cannot sense the emotion of contentment with your current circumstances, what makes you think you will feel it with your desired circumstances? Your desired circumstances will only change your view. Once you get there, you will be subjected to a whole new and higher realm of advertising proclaiming that you can have more than this.

How money makes you feel and influences your perspectives in life often depends on how much or little you have. Money offers arrogance to the "haves" and shame and envy to the "have-nots." Who's better? A good guy who's loaded or a good guy who's scraping by? Isn't being a good guy enough to warrant admiration?

Money won't make you happy, but neither will poverty.
—Warren Buffett

Possessions can be personal rewards for significant labors—and there is certainly nothing wrong with rewarding your efforts. Where many individuals go wrong, however, is in believing that things, once possessed, will make them happy. Ultimately, they will not. In fact, these things have the potential to make you unhappy because all things of value require responsibility and insecurity. A bigger house means more work, more maintenance, and more things that can go wrong—at a bigger price tag. Part of the price tag of that shiny new car, boat, or other luxury item is insecurity, because now there is worry about damage and risk.

When I started making really good money, I decided to buy myself a really nice watch, something in the Rolex genre. In the midst of my search, I stopped myself with the thought that I wasn't really being honest with myself as to why I wanted this watch. I came to the conclusion that the motive I was articulating didn't agree with what I was feeling. I said I wanted the watch because "I wanted a nice-looking, dependable timepiece." But what I was feeling inside was that I simply wanted to impress others with my achievements. I asked myself if I really needed to spend $7,000 to tell everyone I had made it. I thought of some of my family back home who wouldn't know a Rolex from a Timex. I came to a compromise. I decided I did indeed want to reward myself with a fine timepiece but that I would not choose a brand that was a blatant advertisement of my achievement. I bought a brand every bit as beautiful *and dependable as a Rolex but far less recognizable to the masses. This decision started a very powerful line of reasoning that, so far, has kept me from buying a bigger house and more expensive car than I really need and has helped to keep my materialism in check. It's like the old saying, "We buy things we don't need with money we don't have to impress people we don't like." And I'm trying not to go down that path.*

—Doug, insurance executive

Happiness is easy. Don't complicate it. If you want what you have, you are happy.

Fulfillment Is Optimizing Your Abilities

Fulfillment is doing the things you love to do. It is expressing your working soul. It is engaging in work that energizes rather than depletes you. Fulfillment does not necessarily come from success in the career you are in if that career is not the soul-felt expression of who you are. When you are expressing who you are with your work, you have shaken hands with fulfillment. Once you discover this relationship between who you are and what you do, it is awfully difficult to go back to work that engages the hands but not the heart.

I remember the lack of fulfillment I felt at one point in my career because I was doing the same routine over and over. I knew I needed an outlet for the creative impulse within me. I wasn't fulfilled until I found ways to express that creativity. I now know that I can never go back to the kind of work that clogs the creative impulse urging me from within. My first criterion today when I am offered work is not how much I'll make but whether it will be a creative challenge. Once you discover the work that fulfills you, it will be hard, if not impossible, to disengage yourself from it.

Balance Is Walking the Tightrope between Too Much and Not Enough

Work, family, and leisure—when they are in balance, we enjoy life. Feeling as if we're having fun in life is a good indicator that we have achieved some degree of balance. How many people do you know who have worked hard for so long that they no longer know how to relax when they get the opportunity? How many people do you know who are so busy supporting their family that they never actually see their family? What do they achieve by neglecting the very people who motivate them to earn a good living? People today are aware of these issues and are no longer as willing to put their personal life in a deep freeze for the sake of their company's goals. It is becoming a common question among job applicants to ask, "Will I have a life?" A growing percentage of employees are willing to trade more income for more time and flexibility, even during tough economic times.

At the other extreme of the life balance pendulum are individuals who have so much time for leisure that they have lost their sense of purpose and significance, and, consequently, their fun is no longer fun. There is a fine balance to be achieved in attending to the physical, emotional, social, and spiritual sides of our being. There is also a fine balance to be achieved in attending to the working, familial, and frolicking sides of our being.

Satisfaction Is Improving the Quality of Your Efforts and Relationships

Satisfaction is a quality issue. If you are constantly seeking to raise the level of quality in the products and services you are involved with, if you are constantly striving to improve key relationships in your life, and if you are living a thoughtful, self-examined life, you will feel a sense of satisfaction.

When talking to those who feel a sense of dissatisfaction in their life, I see a recurring pattern of lukewarm relationships and lack of conviction about the impact and meaning of their daily work. It is important to look for opportunities to satisfy your need for inner satisfaction at the place you are today before you start believing greener grasses elsewhere will satisfy that appetite. I recently talked with a woman who told me she needed to get back to helping the homeless so she could feel a greater sense of satisfaction about her life. She felt her life was too self-absorbed. I asked her what she did in her job to help others. She thought about it and said that she gave seminars helping women discover financial independence. After she said that, she suddenly realized she was ignoring a great source of inner satisfaction right under her nose. Satisfaction can often be fulfilled by appreciating the things we do now and by striving to do them better. By raising our eyes to a standard of excellence in our efforts we raise our levels of satisfaction. Satisfaction revolves around the quality of our efforts and our relationships.

Security Is Possessing the Freedom to Pursue Your Goals

Whether our goals are anchored in work, family, leisure, or all of the above, we feel a sense of security only when we know we will have the freedom to continue pursuing those goals. People may feel insecure about their job for fear of getting laid off and not being able to pursue the work goals they desire. Others fear they will not have enough assets to be able to pursue the lifestyle they want in their retirement years. Possessing adequate finances can unquestionably provide a degree of security because it can offer a material guarantee, of sorts, that we will be able to do what we want with our lives. This is the security that modern retirement represents for most people. Life will always present us with opportunities to feel insecure because very little in this world is guaranteed. We may have the money to do what we want, but our health could diminish and rob us of our mobility and activity. We can make all sorts of plans for the future, but we have no guarantee that those plans will pan out.

Security hinges on more than just the health of our assets; it is also affected by the health of our body and close relationships. As billionaire Warren Buffett put it, "The only two things that can make you truly happy in this world are people that love you and being healthy, and money can't buy you either one of those." We can, however, build on our sense of security by staying close to those who love us, forming good physical habits, and continuing to put away all we can toward our financial emancipation.

Significance Is Making the Best Use of Your Time

Viktor Frankl stated that man's chief motivation was the need for significance. People are motivated by a need to make a difference somehow in others' lives—to feel they are making a contribution that is significant. Many people erroneously believe that a sense of significance will be satisfied by the acquisition of power and control over others. It cannot. This inward sense of significance is satisfied by the best possible use of our most valuable resource: time.

We all have only so many days on this Earth, and those days are fleeting. Look at how quickly the last decade has seemed to pass. Parents get a magnified perspective on the fleeting nature of time as they watch their children sprout and then launch into their own lives while the mother and father feel almost the same as they did 15 years earlier. People want to make a difference in other people's lives. People want to make a difference in the work they do. People want to make a difference with the wise distribution of their time, energy, and resources. Money has the power to feed this significance only when it is shared or emancipates us to share our time and skills. Charity and volunteerism can be crucial to a sense of significance in our lives.

A person who works in a job but doesn't see the benefit of that job to the end will almost always lack a sense of significance. He will feel that he is wasting his time. A person who is a workaholic and misses all her children's meaningful activities will feel that she is abusing the short time she has. Significance is closely related to how we manage the time we have.

Success Is the Satisfaction of Reaching Your Goals

Success is a sense that relies heavily on moving toward, or achieving, personal goals. But the term *success* must be broadened beyond the material to have real meaning in life. Truly successful individuals have goals involving who they are (character), what they do (career), and what they possess (material)—and, more than likely, in that order of importance. How successful does an individual who is garnering riches but failing in the personal character department feel? Certainly, one's reputation is worth its weight in gold. Financial success could be defined as having enough to meet your own needs and the needs of those you choose to help. This is a worthy financial goal. Career success could be defined as having the opportunity to pursue one's career goals. We feel most successful when we are actively pursuing our heartfelt goals. As long as we are actively pursuing personal goals and making progress toward them, our sense of success and confidence will be fed.

A sense of success starts with first *having* a goal. Many fail the financial success test at this point because they have not clearly defined their financial goals. Having enough to retire is not a goal; it is a vague desire, a dream. Wanting to have financial assets of half a million dollars by the time you are 60 is a clearly articulated goal. Now you have a standard against which to measure your financial success. Having a clearly defined goal to feel successful holds as true in your career and character as in your finances. Studies show that the majority of people do not have clearly defined financial goals, and I would assume this to be true in other areas of life as well. In the financial realm, this problem can be easily remedied by partnering with someone who can first help you articulate those goals and then help you stay the course in achieving those goals.

These seven intangibles cannot be satisfied by a certain amount of material possessions or by a number. Happiness, fulfillment, balance, satisfaction, security, significance, and success should not be the by-products of life; they should be the goals! Having these seven intangibles present in our souls is the very definition of rich living in spite of the amount of our investable assets. When we myopically focus on money instead of meaning in our lives, we deny ourselves the fulfillment that we could garner both from our means and our time. Remember, your life is not about making money—*your money is about making a life.* These seven intangibles cannot be bought, but you can easily sell them out.

The Stewardship of Money

My deepest conviction regarding the topic of important conversations around money is that the conversation is not complete until we examine our relationship to money in the light of stewardship. A definition of the word *steward* is a person whose responsibility is to take care of something: *farmers pride themselves on being stewards of the land.* Stewardship is the transcendent realization that although material wealth is in our care, it is never really "ours." The money is passing through us as if we were conduits.

We don't achieve financial/life success by engaging in a numbers-only money discussion, hoping that it fits our lives. We experience financial/life success by taking a closer look at our lives—what we are experiencing, what we hope to experience—and by designing a financial plan around those life factors. What can you do to make a meaningful and resourceful transition in your life? Begin by following these three steps:

1. Decide what is *meaningful* in your life.
2. Begin looking at innovative ways to use your resources (money, time, and ability) to pursue the life you want.
3. Partner with those people who can help you articulate and achieve your goals.

Ultimately, living "rich" is about aligning your life and money—by placing meaning at the center of each financial decision. It is what I call *investing on purpose.* Once you adopt this approach, you may find a new sense of wholeness and peace surrounding your financial and investment decisions because you are engaging in *a unifying philosophy of life that defines purpose for your money and, consequently, your life.*

CHAPTER

Maslow Meets Retirement

*Self-actualization is the desire to become more and more what one
is, to become everything that one is capable of becoming.*
                                                        —Abraham Maslow

My friend Teddy gets up every day at 4 a.m. He's at the gym working out by 5:15. He then goes home and catches up on reading the papers online. Then he goes to one of his businesses for breakfast. Then he checks on his other businesses. Then he goes to play a round of golf (walking) then . . . I'm getting tired just reiterating this guy's schedule. Oh, by the way, Teddy is in his mid-70s, going on 45.

Teddy shares some very candid feedback with me from time to time about people his age. "Too many complainers. I don't like complaining, and I don't want to hear it!" is one sample. Another is an economic observation. Teddy winters on the east coast of Florida in an area that attracts wealthy retirees. "These people have all the money in the world and don't know how to spend it." Teddy in years past also shared with me what I consider to be my absolute favorite thought on spending: "The only money that's really yours is the money you spend. Everything else goes to somebody else." Touché.

I was recently on a speaking tour in Ireland and spent a half day with retirement planners learning about the issues they observed with their clients. At the top of their list were two items:

1. People wanting a real purpose in retirement; and
2. People being free to spend what they worked so hard to gain.

Ironic isn't it? We are all creatures of habit. It has been said that "the chains of habit are too light to be felt until they are too heavy to remove." This apparently applies to our spending habits as well. Some of you may be reading this and thinking, "I wish that was my problem," or "I wish I had enough so I could have that problem!" but this chapter is about finding a correlation between what matters most in life and how we disperse our assets. This is an alignment that is as good for the soul's purpose as it is for the purse.

More Than Just Money

At the age of 52, Briggs Matsko was about to retire from his financial planning business. A friend heard about Briggs's plans and sent him a copy of this book. Briggs said that reading *The New Retirementality* not only changed his life but also gave him a new passion and mission for the work he thought he was going to leave.

I had the pleasure of meeting Briggs over breakfast while in California on a speaking engagement. He shared this story with me:

> I had a real epiphany when I read your book and realized that the most foolish thing I could do is retire early and go into a life of wondering how to make a difference. The opportunity for making a difference was right there in front of me in every client conversation. I just needed to change the conversation from being a numbers conversation to being a life conversation.

We first need to figure out what we desire out of life and then how we are going to pay for it—find it first and then fund it. The idea is not to arrange our finances first and then see if we can find a life within that framework. In fact, it is the opposite: figure out the life you want and organize your financial situation to serve that purpose.

With a desire to facilitate a money dialogue revolving around what people desire out of life, I created a financial conversation called "Income for Life," where I overlaid Abraham Maslow's

Hierarchy of Needs with a financial inquiry. I mentioned this idea to Briggs at our breakfast that morning, and I thought he was going to jump out of his chair. His eyes got as big as the over-easy eggs on his plate, and it was obvious that he just had to tell me something.

"What is it, Briggs?" I asked. "Are you familiar with Maslow's model?"

"One of the first things I did when coming back to work with my new vision," Briggs spilled out, "was to create an income dialogue with clients that I called 'Matsko's Hierarchy of Needs,' where we look at a client's emotional needs before making financial decisions." Briggs confessed, regarding the play with Maslow's name, "I just couldn't resist, with our names being so similar and all."

Briggs had intuitively settled on the same solution as I did after adopting *The New Retirementality*—an income plan designed to simultaneously settle both emotional and financial ledgers.

Briggs and I had both independently observed that, too often, financial advice and financial planning are based on numbers and strategies outside of the very context they are intended to address: quality of life and a sense of emotional well-being. People cannot simply numbers-crunch their way to emotional well-being and quality of life, but neither can they achieve these ends without crunching the numbers and making the necessary adjustments. There is a need for a *financial life planning* approach amalgamating both realms into one conversation.

According to the 2017 *Generations Ahead Study*, more Americans are afraid of living than dying! Sixty-two percent of us are more afraid we'll run out of money in retirement than we are of facing death.[1] People are mortally afraid of living to be 100 and being poor. This socioeconomic anxiety, "bag-lady/poor-old-man syndrome" is deeply rooted in the fear of outliving our money. With the confluence of an aging revolution, rising health care costs, and the erosive power of inflation on our money, it is easy to see how people may not be optimistic about their later years.

As a young man in Iowa, I worked with a social worker named Jeannie to create a charity for widows in our town who were living on minimal food and heat in the winter months. Jeannie discovered the problem by talking to grocery store clerks who said little old ladies were buying dog food, when it was known they did not even own a pet. Jeannie began walking the streets. When she found an older house in somewhat disheveled condition, she would knock on the door and ask to visit. What she found was appalling.

During the winter little old ladies would answer the door in full winter gear because they had to turn their heat down to 55 degrees or risk having it turned off by the power company for nonpayment. Those who chose to heat neglected to eat, or they ate dog food, as Jeannie stealthily discovered by checking their cupboards. These women were too indoctrinated in Depression-era self-sufficiency to ask for assistance, and so we had to find creative ways to help them (e.g., anonymously paying their heating bills). This experience has stayed with me 30-plus years in a visceral way—I don't want to be old and poor. None of us does.

Our Hierarchy of Financial Needs

We will all eventually need to engage in a conversation about developing an income stream that lasts as long as we do, outpacing the inflation that threatens to rot our nest egg slowly but surely. To accomplish this task, let's begin looking at Maslow's Hierarchy of Needs (with money in mind) and walk through the process of designing an income for life. I have developed a slightly altered financial rendition of Maslow's Hierarchy of Needs for this purpose (see Figure 13.1).

Maslow taught that human beings are motivated by unmet needs, and that lower needs must be satisfied before the higher needs can be addressed. We must meet people's most basic needs (like physical survival) before they will be able to address other needs (like love or actualization). Rather than study rats (like Skinner) or the mentally ill and neurotic (like Freud), Maslow developed his theory by studying people such as Albert Einstein, Eleanor Roosevelt, and Frederick Douglass. The hierarchy Maslow offered was physical survival, safety, love, esteem, and self-actualization.

For the purposes of a financial/life discussion, I have taken the liberty of renaming and juxtaposing two categories: love and esteem. Love, in Maslow's definition, had to do with belonging—to a spouse, to a family, to a community, or to a group. For a financial discussion, I have titled this area "gifting," as this is most often the material expression of love.

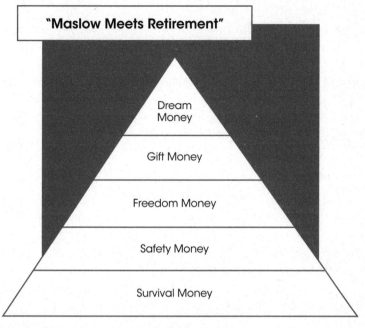

Figure 13.1   Maslow Meets Retirement

What Maslow called *esteem*, I have called *freedom* in the financial/ life hierarchy. Maslow was referring to the self-esteem that results from doing things well and being recognized for the doing. In the Income for Life model, this is categorized under "freedom money" because unless people have the freedom to do what they want with their occupational lives, they will be missing the esteem and satisfaction that come from doing what they are best at. How many people do you know who long to apply themselves occupationally to something they are naturally good at?

There is also an aspect of financial freedom that allows us to address not just esteem but enjoyment as well. Hobbies and trips and exploration cost money, and if we don't prepare an income stream to address these costs, we may not realize those experiences. I have placed freedom below gifting on the hierarchy because, from a financial point of view, it is quite unlikely that we will give money away to others *before* we are free to pursue a fulfilling life ourselves. However, there are exceptions to this rule, such as the case of parents who slave at jobs they hate in order to pay for a college education for their children. I happen to believe, however, that it is far healthier—from both emotional and financial perspectives—for people to secure their own freedom to pursue the lives they want. The kids can help with their college expenses by working and saving also.

Following are the phases of financial preparation we need for Income for Life planning.

Survival Income

Survival income is money that we have to have to make ends meet. How much do you need to simply survive each month? $3,000? $7,000? If you stripped away the frills and thrills and just paid the bills of survival, what would it cost? The majority of people have never taken the time to answer this most basic financial question: What is the cost of survival? The money needed to pay for your basic necessities is your survival income.

Safety Income

Safety income is money we must have to meet life's unexpected turns. What if everything doesn't work out as you hoped and imagined it would? In life, the one thing we can predict with great assurance is that things will rarely go exactly as planned. It has been said that "life is what happens while we are making plans." We are surrounded by risks—physical, familial, financial, circumstantial, and relational. Financial risks exist in every category of our lives. Look at the financial risk associated with a divorce: hastens financial ruin, guarantees your assets will be cut in half, and diminishes your saving capacity.

Look at the risk of being disabled for a prolonged period of time. Forty-eight percent of mortgage foreclosures are due to the disability of the chief breadwinner, versus only 3% due to the death of the breadwinner. A person who is 32 years old has 6.5 times the odds that they will be disabled than the odds that they will die before age 65.[2]

As stated earlier, a leading risk in the minds of those individuals approaching retirement is the risk of outliving their money. Other top-of-mind risks are health (and paying for health care), investment risk, loss of income, and financial needs within the family. As much as is possible, we want to protect ourselves against catastrophes to our bodies, our money, and our material things. In many cases, as with our material possessions, this can be accomplished with insurance. It would behoove us all to get an objective opinion on the level of insurance we are carrying toward death, disability, and catastrophe. One incident can wipe out a lifetime of earning. The money needed to guard against these risks is your safety income.

Freedom Income

Freedom income is money to do all of the things that bring enjoyment and fulfillment to life. What is the exact cost of the activities and indulgences that bring pleasure and relaxation into your life? Some people engage in low-cost relaxation activities (like walking), and others engage in high-priced activities (like walking after a golf ball at a private club). Travel, adventure, and personal growth/education are also some of the considerations to include when calculating the amount needed to fund your freedom.

Gift Income

Gift income is money for the people and causes that we care deeply about. As we move up Maslow's pyramid—securing our survival, safety, and freedom—our money can be utilized in the higher calling of bringing blessing to those people and causes we care deeply about. If you are a part of what has been characterized as "the sandwich generation," you are experiencing financial concerns on both ends of the generational spectrum. Many of us would love to do something for our parents *and* our children. Many of us also have aspirations to support causes and charities that connect with our heart and purpose. The money needed to pay for these gifts and benevolent annuities is your gifting income.

Dream Income

Dream income is money for the things we've always dreamed of being, doing, and having. Some would call it their "bucket list" money—borrowing from the movie of the same title starring Jack Nicholson. What do you want to be? What do you want to do? What do you want to have? These are all part of the financial conversation necessary for paying the bills of self-actualization. For some people, only a career change will bring them to this place. For others, it may require part-time involvement in activities more closely aligned with their sense of passion and purpose.

The cost of self-actualization is the time it takes to do the things that bring meaning into our lives. If we do not own enough of our own time to engage in these activities, then we must negotiate with our work schedule and personal finances to make the time available. There is often a cost associated with being what we want to be.

There are also costs associated with doing what we want to do and having what we want to have. Some of us dream of owning a sailboat and spending a year sailing from port to port. Others dream of owning a recreational vehicle and seeing America. Whatever dreams and adventures have surfaced in your own musings on self-actualization, there will be bills to pay in the process. The money needed to pay these bills is your dream income.

Paying the Bills

The final phase of the *income for life* discussion is to match your income sources against your income needs—which sources will pay for which needs (see Figure 13.2, *Income/Outcome Worksheet*). If it's a case of having only enough to pay for survival and safety at this point, then you will at least have the comfort of knowing those two critical bases are covered.

You will also have a clear picture of how much you will need to meet your other needs. You can then set goals around saving and budgeting to expedite achieving the income necessary for funding these important needs of freedom, gifts, and actualization. As one financial planner stated: "If your outgo exceeds your income, you may need to downsize to realize your upside." In other words, if your income isn't enough to meet your needs, you may have to negotiate with your needs.

Get a handle on what you need and what you have. This exercise produces clarity. Get a handle on what you need to do to get

Match your various sources to the income category you want them to pay for.

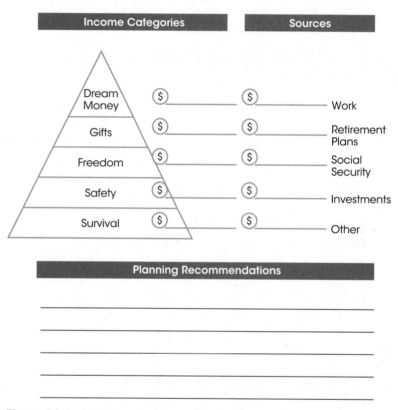

Figure 13.2   Income/Outcome Worksheet

what you want, and how long it will take to get there. This exercise also brings hope. Begin to view your income not as just a way to pay the bills but as a means to funding a life—the life *you* want.

CHAPTER

Advice from Retirementors

*Simplicity is the most difficult thing to secure in this world; it is
the last limit of experience and the last effort of genius.*

—George Sand

In 2018 I worked on a unique study sponsored by Invesco Consulting Group. The study looked at three key retirement dynamics: location, vocation, and vacation. The purpose of the study was to survey those who had been retired an average of seven years, in order to determine what was—and wasn't—working for them. We wanted to get insights from participants who might be willing to pass on their retirement life lessons to those planning toward, or just embarking upon, retirement. We figured that from this size of sample group we were bound to find some *retirementors.*

The study surveyed 500 retirees who had $500,000 to $3,000,000 in investible assets (i.e., real estate was not included): 68% of the participants were from the private sector, 22% were from the government sector, and 10% were from the nonprofit sector. In this chapter, we'll look at what we learned, including some interesting anecdotes participants shared.

The Realities of Retirement

Through the study, we hoped to discover how retirees had negotiated the balancing act of purposeful (vocation) and recreational (vacation) activities. For purposes of the study, vacation was broadly defined as travel, hobbies, and recreational pursuits.

We found that more than a quarter of participants (27%) described hobbies as "just something to do" —implying a lack of visceral engagement or satisfaction with the activities they participated in.

Invesco Consulting Group was interested in finding out whether or not it would be beneficial for financial advisors to establish "Retirementor Councils" within their practices to act as sounding boards or mentors for those who had questions about the realities of retirement. Interestingly, approximately half the respondents indicated an interest in such a concept while the other half had little or no interest.

Participants reported that "financial planning" was the top area they would have enjoyed learning about before retirement, followed almost equally by "maintaining mental acuity" and "travel opportunities":

Financial planning	76%
Maintaining mental acuity	45%
Travel opportunities	43%
Maintaining health	39%
Incorporating volunteer work into retirement	39%
Maintaining purpose	36%
Maintaining social/family connections	19%
Changing location	18%
Engaging in sports/hobbies	16%
How do issues that are important to you compare to these results?	

Almost half the participants (48%) reported turning to a financial advisor for advice regarding planning for the future, followed by aging experts (46%), retired friends or family members (36%), or anyone already retired (25%).

More than three quarters (77%) of participants felt they were prepared. What's interesting is that the top reason reported for feeling ready was because they had reached their "number"—this response demonstrates how narrow our view of retirement readiness really is:

Hit my number/financially prepared	30%
Conducted research/knew what to expect	20%
Maintained my health/kept fit/still physically active	16%
Talked with friends/family who are retired to learn from their experiences	4%
Did a practice run at retiring before permanently retiring	2%

Those who did not feel prepared (23%) cited underestimating the lifestyle benefits of working as their top factor for unpreparedness. It's also important to note that, for the respondents who reported being unprepared, just about a quarter experienced an event they hadn't expected, and an almost equal number of participants didn't feel that they had the support system necessary to make the transition.

Be sure to forecast both what you expect and don't expect as an important part of successful planning:

Did not think through giving up the benefits of working (i.e., sense of purpose, camaraderie, etc.)	32%
Experienced an unexpected life event in retirement	24%
Did not do a practice run at retiring before permanently retiring	23%
Do not have many retired friends/family members to learn from or turn to for support	22%
Did not maintain health/keep physically active	18%
Did not adequately research/did not know what to expect	10%
Did not use a financial advisor to develop a financial game plan	11%
Didn't hit their number/was not financially prepared	7%

When asked the follow-up question, "Why do you think you retired too soon?," "Underestimating the value of work" was the leading answer (41%), followed by "More expensive than anticipated" (15%), "Boredom" (12%), and "Having spouse/friends who were not retired" (12%). As these results indicate, work is more than simply a paycheck, even if we don't realize it at the time.

More than half the participants (56%) reported that financial advisors were their primary source for insights on retirement. Social media ranked the lowest:

Financial advisor	56%
General information on Internet	41%
Advice from people already retired	41%
Books and magazines	31%
Social media	3%

Having multiple sources of advice can help you ensure a plan that is unique to you.

Retiremyths

One unintended result of the study was discovering a number of what we labeled *retiremyths*—assumptions that many people have about retirement, most of which turned out not to be true with our participants:

The Retiremyth	The Truth
Retirees go back to school	Only 7% thought about it
Retirees relocate	Only 25% moved
Retiring means you are no longer working	At least 25% work full or part time
Expenses decrease in retirement	37% indicated that expenses did not decrease; in fact, many indicated they actually increased

We'll read a lot more about the perception-versus-reality of retirement as we look at issues surrounding location, vocation, vacation, and allocation.

Location: Should I Stay or Should I Go?

Almost all participants (96%) who did move were satisfied or very satisfied with their decision, and 84% of those who didn't move were satisfied or very satisfied with their decision. So, if you're asking—or singing along with The Clash, "Should I stay or should I go?," odds are in your favor either way. Just be sure you do it for the right reasons.

Those who stayed said they did so for family and friends and/or because they enjoyed their house, city, and/or neighborhood. Those who moved said they did so for better weather or to be closer to family—some got both. A majority (71%) moved out of state while a minority moved locally (8%). While expenses and taxes were reasons to move, they were secondary to weather and being close to family and friends:

Wanted to live in better climate/weather	44%
To be closer to friends/family members	35%
New location is known to be retiree-friendly	33%
Current location too expensive	28%
Taxes in current location too high	26%
Wanted a change of pace	24%
Relocated in different area, but in the same state	20%
Always wanted to live in new location	18%
New location has good medical facilities	15%
New location has similar political views as me	12%

We uncovered some unexpected observations in the "Location" section of the study:

"The new political climate causes me to be at odds with others."

"California is very liberal, and taxes are excessive!"

"Left a corrupt state run by idiots."

"My wife no longer drives because of lack of familiarity with location."

"My biggest issue is finding new friends. Have been working on that."

"Don't move to be near children or grandchildren. They are free to relocate and often do, leaving you to decide whether to move again."

These observations are reminders that neighbors are important at the micro and the macro levels. It's critical that you think about all aspects of where you are relocating to—and do your homework before the moving van pulls up.

Vocation: The Role of Purpose in Retirement

Volunteering proved to provide the biggest purpose payoff for those who engaged as volunteers, but 60% of the study participants did not volunteer. A quarter of those said they "were too busy to have time to help others." So if a retiree is feeling a waning sense of purpose at any point, it might be worth exploring the roles they could play in the nonprofit sector. The study also found that the purpose/passion payoff of volunteering was twice that of what hobbies provided for those who answered the question. Volunteering also proved to be an effective path to forming new relationships, on par with meeting people at neighborhood events or through existing friends.

Neighborhood activities/community centers:	52%
Social events/through existing friends:	48%
Volunteer activities:	43%
Sports/hobbies:	42%
Church/religious activities:	33%
Educational pursuits:	5%

Volunteering is not for everyone, but it is a good way to engage with your community, meet new people, and have a sense of purpose. Some unexpected observations included having one's schedule hijacked and hard-earned spontaneity threatened by volunteer activities. My observation has been that nonprofits typically don't seek out people with little to do; instead, they deliberately look for already-busy volunteers because they know they'll be more focused and productive.

Many participants chose to work part time for the lifestyle benefits, including socializing, feeling productive, and being intellectually engaged and challenged. Their observations skewed physical, mental, fiscal, and relational well-being:

"Pick flexible hours."
"Don't count on being able to work; health problems can easily intervene."
"Try to line up post-retirement work while still employed."
"Your knowledge is still valuable."

"Back away slowly."

"Do some soul searching: try out some of things during week-ends or vacations to see if they really fit."

"Avoid quitting all at once: a slower transition through part-time work allows better adjustment to having more free time and to learning to live without a regular paycheck."

Interestingly, very few tried practice runs at retirement but those that did (97%) found them to be beneficial.

Instead of simply jumping off a cliff into retirement, think of ways you can transition into a lifestyle that works for *you.*

Find Your Spot

The engagements participants chose were varied, both in terms of what they did and how much time they committed. Some worked in fields for the perks gained, whereas others just slowed down the pace of what they had done in their careers:

"I work at a golf course one day a week to get a little spending money and free golf privileges."

"Short-term contracts."

"Project-based work."

"Consulting."

"Teaching."

"Art as a second career."

"Real estate as a second career."

"Part-time ski instructor."

"Counsel people in other states on how to manage their ill-nesses and financial difficulties."

In the *Vocation* part of the study, finding ways to maintain passion for life was a frequently mentioned goal. This is especially true for people whose entire identity and fulfillment was based on their career:

"Have passion for things other than work. You definitely need a reason to get up every morning."

"Do what you love and help others."

"Find things that energize you."

"Pick something you can get excited about, not just something to keep busy."

"Enjoy every day like it was your last; you have no guarantees on life and how long you will live."

Watch Your "Bored-O-Meter"

Some participants reported boredom setting in. They commented on being disengaged mentally and sedentary physically:

"It can get boring not having people around to talk with."

"Do not retire to just sit on your backside; keep active physically and mentally."

"Too much time at beginning but started reconnecting with people."

"Time moves slowly if one is not actively involved in something interesting."

"When not traveling, too much dead time."

"Sometimes boring and you develop bad habits: Internet, TV, eating out."

"Bored; I needed to look for activities to keep busy."

In the questions around vocation, we asked participants about the role work plays for those who have retired in the past decade or so. If current trends play out, a quarter of you who retire will return to work—and not just because you may need the money. Needing a sense of purpose—something to wake up and show up for—was twice as important as earning money:

Needed a purpose/sense of accomplishment	67%
Wanted more social interaction	56%
Wanted to stay engaged/maintain mental acuity	44%
Underestimated financial needs	33%
Other	22%

It's interesting to note that more than half of the participants returned to work within a year (56%) while less than a quarter (22%) returned after being out of work between three and five years and 11% returned after being out of work one to three years. My interpretation of the data is that most people realized they missed working soon after retiring, or they got bored after a few years of nothing but leisure.

Vacation: Balancing Work and Play

Participants responding to the Vacation portion of the survey reported that it was important to explore the possibilities, but also to be aware of the limitations of all play, all the time:

"Combine volunteering with play."

"Downscale how you play so you have funds to still enjoy."

"Leisure is important. But don't think that leisure is all you will want."

"You will miss the social aspect of your work life."

"You may need to keep some structure in your day. I find that time slips away from me some days, and I need anchors— gym, choir practice, freelance gigs—to keep me productive."

"Lack of companionship/difficulty meeting new friends" came up consistently as problems with *Vacation* (travel and leisure activities)— there were multiple comments about not being able to vacation because of a lack of money, health issues, and responsibility for a pet or house.

Those who had backloaded their travel and were connecting with friends and family were satisfied with their freedom and flexibility. They enjoyed their latitude to be able to visit friends in various parts of the country, and to use the reward points they had accrued, combined with timeshares and Airbnb properties.

There were some comments that too much vacation can become boring: your personal threshold for leisure time versus other engagements will have an impact on how you spend your time. Not everyone wants to be on a permanent vacation, as enticing as that may sound.

Many of the respondents encountered unexpected obstacles, including loss of spouse, disability, or caretaking:

> "Became a widow. Hard to find a travel companion."
> "Never expected my disability."
> "I don't take vacations since I don't want to leave my dogs with someone else."
> "Having to care for a parent who has Alzheimer's."

One person made the interesting comment that, "[I] actually have less leisure time now than when I worked because of less structured work hours," which we assumed to mean that because they were on an on-call, part-time work schedule, they had a harder time scheduling leisure activities than they did with a predictable work schedule.

Affordability

Participants brought up some interesting financial issues:

> "Beware of the cost of leisure!"
> "Guilt. Major vacations are more expensive than I'm willing to pay. Some of that is my fear of wasting resources I might need later."
> "My husband is not available to do the things I want to do, now that I'm retired, because he has to continue to work, to pay the bills."

Bucket Listers

It seems like Jack Nicholson and Morgan Freeman's 2007 movie *Bucket List* has inspired many of us to create and pursue our own bucket lists. "Do it while you know you can" seems to be the theme here. We were told about varying and diverse adventures and experiences such as:

> "A tour of the USA with our camper."
> "A trip to South Africa, complete with a safari."
> "Baseball Hall of Fame."

"Break 80 one more time at golf."

"Do a gorilla trek in Uganda."

"Family reunion in Wisconsin."

"Get a Tesla."

"Go to the US Open tennis tournament to see Serena Williams play."

"Helicopter skiing, now that I am a much better skier than the first time I tried it on my 50th birthday."

"I have visited 49 states, need to finish."

"Jumping out of an airplane."

"Go to Karaoke."

"Return trip to Vietnam."

"See a Green Bay Packers game at Lambeau field."

I had to include this last item as I'm a lifelong Packers fan (even though my family follows another team clothed in purple). Everyone loved the Lambeau experience! As you can see, everyone's bucket list is different.

What's on your bucket list? Be sure to include the cost of bucket list items in your planning.

The Best (and Worst) Experiences

The best experiences people cited included everything from relationships to freedom from certain responsibilities. On the relational front, many found new fonts of joy in family: "Being able to be in my grandchildrens' lives every day. It's the best thing!" and, "Being able to connect with a family member that I only previously heard about."

Regarding the newfound freedom from certain responsibilities, comments included, "The best experience I have had in retirement is the overwhelming sense of freedom and lack of work-related responsibility. It's just given me a whole new outlook on life," as well as, "No bosses: being able to go where I choose, when I choose, and do whatever I like to do."

Many talked about finding more time to enjoy the outdoors: "Getting my $10 national parks pass and being able drive from one to another taking pictures," and "Sitting on my back porch, smoking my cigar, watching a family of deer, including two very young ones, eat my bushes and grass." We couldn't tell if he was amused or annoyed by the deer—probably a bit of both.

When respondents were asked about their biggest regrets, answers ranged from purely economic to introspective:

The financial regrets ranged from the tongue-in-cheek—"Not being born into the 1%"—to those who wished they had saved more money before retiring and been more cautious with their spending. Some said they wished they had finished their home improvement projects before they had retired while others cited home improvement as an activity they had looked forward to.

Some rued not having the help of a financial planner, especially regarding taxes, and the Rubik's Cube of required minimum distributions, Social Security options, and estate planning. One respondent commented, "I wish I had better understood what life in retirement could look like and tried to better understand all my options. I also wish I had paid closer attention to my health."

What can you do now to prepare for your future?

Allocation

A third of participants (33%) reported feeling guilty about spending money in retirement. Apparently, it's not easy to flip the switch from disciplined saving to enjoying the spoils of your labors. Other concerns included health care costs (37%) and anxiety about expenses being higher than expected (36%).

Participants in the study talked about being surprised with other financial factors as well, including getting paid once a month instead of more often, the complexity of managing required minimum distributions, the relief they felt from having paid off their mortgage, and how much more fiscally conservative they became after retiring:

"Absolutely no gambling away your money."
"Health savings account, 401(k), and state pension kept retirement stress free."
"Thankful for that inheritance."
"Prepare a budget and stick to it."

"Put yourself first, deal with passing wealth later."

"Be sure you can afford it."

"Be sure your financial house is in order and that you have paid down any debt so that you can have a budget that allows you to do all the things you want to do."

"My expenses shifted but did not decrease."

"Don't spend money foolishly; every penny adds up."

"Did not realize my family would need as much help financially."

"Divorce has had a big negative impact on finances."

"I put too much faith in a 401(k); now it's time to pay for that."

"Investment interest rates fell more than I thought."

"Trying to monitor it all ourselves. Too complicated."

"Make sure you have a fiduciary for a financial advisor."

"As the house ages, there is more upkeep that needs to be done."

The S.O.R.R.Y. Factor

The timing of your retirement matters as much as the amount in your retirement account. If your retirement happens to synchronize with a major market meltdown or recession, you're going to have some interesting challenges. When we asked, "What did not work for you financially?" some reported that they had been victimized by what the financial planning profession calls *Sequence of Return Risk*, or what I call the S.O.R.R.Y. factor—Sequence of Return Risk Y'all. Simply put, this is about how the timing of your retirement correlates with the timing of a major correction in the markets. A person who retired in the summer of 2008 and largely invested in the stock market knows the sharp pangs of sequence of returns risk.

Very few people have the resources to withstand the correlation of their retirement nest-egg getting cut in half against inflating prices for living. It's the veritable two-edged fiscal sword. None of us has prophetic insight into what will happen next, so managing our investment risk is a major consideration going into retirement. This doesn't mean all your money needs to be tied up in guaranteed annuities, but it does mean you need to know how much market correction you can tolerate with the lifestyle you're living. If you're working with a financial advisor, he or she should be able to walk you through this before you make the move into a place with no more paychecks. If you're managing on your own, you'll need to make sure you allow for as much margin as possible between your cost of living and the income that you're relying on from your investments. If you're in a position where a serious market protection causes a major disruption in your lifestyle, then you have to either recalibrate your lifestyle expenses or extend your time in the workplace.

Attitudinal Factors

Another interesting finding of the study was how participants felt about gaining new experiences, forming new friendships, aging, feeling useful, and more—what we defined as "attitudinal factors." Here are some of the results:

77% felt they were open to new experiences.
74% said they felt useful.
67% said they were comfortable with getting older.
59% have made new friends.
52% attempted to balance contributions and enjoying themselves.

The study had an awful lot to say about balancing the books, both literally and figuratively. You'll want to find the comfort zone between your intended lifestyle and financial flow, as well as between taking it easy and living with purpose. Therein lies the challenges from both the fiscal and the philosophical points of view.

CHAPTER

From Aging to S-Aging

There is in the act of preparing the moment we start caring.
—Winston Churchill

I often ask audiences if they know someone who is 75 years old and acts like he is 35 and see appreciative nods. I then ask if they know someone who is 45 who acts like she is 80 and see the eyes roll and the knowing nods. The question I then like to pose is this: What, then, are we saying about one's "real age" and the aging process? We are assenting to the idea that, though one's age is a matter of chronology, aging itself is largely a matter of attitude. There can be a wide disparity between being a certain age and acting out that age—hence the phrase "You're as young as you think." The fact that we know 75-year-olds who act 45 affirms the attitudinal and spiritual source that separates those who are aging from those who are old.

Old isn't what it used to be. Remember that when the age for retirement was originally set at 65, a majority of people didn't even live until retirement age. Now we live 20 to 30 years past the retirement age. The age of 65 today has little resemblance to the age of 65 in, say, 1990. Most people are not old at 65 today. They may or may not have slowed down. Thirty years ago you didn't see many men in their 70s and 80s jumping out of airplanes, flying in outer space, or riding skateboards. You may recall the story I shared earlier about the four generations of family members who water ski together: great-grandpa at 92, grandpa at 63, dad at 40, and junior at 5! Seniors of the future will pursue similar active lifestyles. We will see more and more role models of advanced years in years to come.

It is ironic that our society, rather than adjusting to this longevity trend, continues to promote a retirement age that was established over 125 years ago. Many have failed to comprehend that if they retire at 60, for example, they could spend as many years in their retirement as they did in their working career. This is great if you have some invigorating and challenging pursuits before you in those 30-plus years. If you don't, history shows that you'll never see those 30 extra years.

How old will you be when you really become old? It seems that the answer to that question is as individual as the person answering it. We know that the marker for old is no longer 65. Some recent surveys show that most seniors now feel that the marker for old is somewhere nearer 80. Expect that number to keep moving up.

While one finds company in himself and his pursuits, he cannot feel old, no matter what his years may be.

—Amos Alcott

Most people feel that "old" is defined by a decline in mental or physical abilities while less than half feel it is defined by age. Years ago, author Dr. Michael F. Roizen wrote a *New York Times* best seller entitled *Real Age* that enlarged on this idea of locating each individual's "real age," which is the true reflection of one's physical and mental state.[1] After poring over 25,000 medical studies, Roizen and his associates came to the conclusion that age is much more than a chronological marker. Dr. Roizen presents physical, mental, and lifestyle criteria by which each individual can gauge his or her own aging process. In fact, Roizen and his associates came up with over 100 different health behaviors, ranging from diet to stress control, that enable you to assess your real age. More than a chronological marker, age is really the rate at which your internal guardians of health—cardiovascular and immune systems—decline. There is much we can do to slow that decline.

A Sense of Mastery

A MacArthur Foundation study on aging, featured in the book *Successful Aging*, described how one ages successfully. The researchers used the phrase "a sense of mastery" to describe how individuals must believe in their ability to influence events and control their outcomes to be positive and productive in their later years. They found that during a period of less than three years, those who increased their sense of mastery also increased their productivity. The opposite also held true—those whose sense of personal mastery decreased saw a significant reduction in their involvement in productive activities.[2] The findings have held up. In fact, in his 2018 book, *Better with Age: The Psychology of Successful Aging*, Dr. Alan D. Castel reports on the latest research that shows how some people age well while others don't—it's all about striving to be your best by balancing psychological health with remaining physically active—in other words, personal mastery.[3] What exactly is personal mastery? It is self-reliance.

What exactly does it take to become more self-reliant and shift your life into a higher state of confidence and healthy, active living? Three important factors come into play:

1. An opportunity to undertake a specific action that challenges one's sense of self-sufficiency without overwhelming it.
2. The presence of supporting and reassuring others.
3. The experience of succeeding at something with confirming feedback from others.

A sense of confidence works on the same dynamics at any age. We imagine ourselves doing something. We muster the courage and abandon our inhibitions to try it. We look for feedback for our efforts from the people around us. A historical pitfall of aging is the narrowed radius of the comfort zones that can control a person at age 65. "I've never done that," "I don't know anything about computers," and "I'm too old to start that now!" are examples of verbal indicators that the fossilizing process is already under way. The fact that you often hear 50-year-old people making such statements is proof that "old" can start at any age.

The MacArthur Foundation study mirrors Dr. Castel's findings; both conclude that the three indicators of successful aging are:

1. Avoiding disease and disability.
2. Maintaining mental and physical function.
3. Continuing engagement with life.

More than 20 years later, the findings of this landmark study still apply. Many factors come into play in order to age successfully. The physical, intellectual, social, and spiritual aspects of our being must be attended to equally if we hope to hold back the hands of time. We can readily observe the effect of not attending to one or more of these areas in the lives of people we know who practiced such negligence. It does not take long for the aging process to kick into high gear if we let down our guards of discipline and purposefulness.

The first key to aging successfully is to take an interest in yourself. It doesn't take long in the company of elderly people to figure out which ones are feeling sorry for themselves and which ones are extracting every ounce of life's possibilities. Those who succeed are self-respecting enough to keep their bodies fit, their minds challenged, and their hearts engaged.

Figure out how old you *truly* are in mind and body, and introduce yourself to people who are defying the so-called limitations of age. These individuals have not bought into the idea that they need to move aside for the next generation—or anyone else for that matter. They will leave the race when they are good and ready.

The Vitamin Cs of Successful Aging

Gerontological studies from the past 40 years have turned up a number of factors that correlate with aging well. I've been taking notes as these studies have emerged. I was mildly entertained to see that five of the key factors correlating with aging successfully start with the letter *C*, and so I created the following self-assessment titled the Vitamin Cs of Successful Aging that you can use to rate yourself and your lifestyle. This profile features the following factors:

- Vitamin C1: Connectivity
- Vitamin C2: Challenge
- Vitamin C3: Curiosity
- Vitamin C4: Creativity
- Vitamin C5: Charity

Go ahead and see where you stand with the factors that will help you age successfully.

From Aging To S-Aging

"Aging reflects the relationship of time on our being. Aging describes, in large part, the state of our body. Old, on the other hand, describes our state of mind. It has always been a matter of great interest to me to discover the spiritual and attitudinal aquifer that supplies the fountain of youth." —Mitch Anthony

The 5 Attitudes of Successful Aging

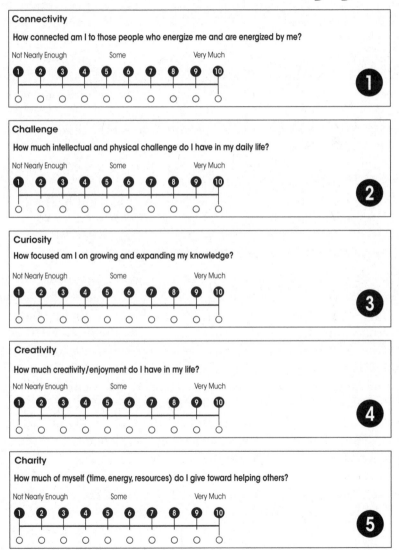

Connectivity

How connected am I to those people who energize me and are energized by me?

Not Nearly Enough   Some   Very Much

1 2 3 4 5 6 7 8 9 10

1

Challenge

How much intellectual and physical challenge do I have in my daily life?

Not Nearly Enough   Some   Very Much

1 2 3 4 5 6 7 8 9 10

2

Curiosity

How focused am I on growing and expanding my knowledge?

Not Nearly Enough   Some   Very Much

1 2 3 4 5 6 7 8 9 10

3

Creativity

How much creativity/enjoyment do I have in my life?

Not Nearly Enough   Some   Very Much

1 2 3 4 5 6 7 8 9 10

4

Charity

How much of myself (time, energy, resources) do I give toward helping others?

Not Nearly Enough   Some   Very Much

1 2 3 4 5 6 7 8 9 10

5

Vitamin C1: Connectivity

The Italian island of Sardinia has 10 times as many centenarians as North America. According to psychologist Susan Pinker, it's not because they all have sunny dispositions or practice low-fat, gluten-free diets. The reason for their longevity is their emphasis on close personal relationships and face-to-face interactions.[4] Why do people retire and immediately move away to a place where they have no social connectivity? Not only are they disconnecting from a major lifeline in the science of successful aging, they might also find out they are annoyed by the culture and accents of the region into which they moved. It might be wise to spend some time doing reconnaissance on the geography and culture where you plan on staging the next act of your life. Many people disconnect themselves from important social networks when they retire and don't realize this until it's too late.

Stay connected to people you love, people you enjoy, and people who appreciate you and see value in your presence. Longevity does not favor the Lone Ranger. Both long life and happiness are tied to the quality of your connections.

Vitamin C2: Challenge (Intellectual and Physical)

The latest Alzheimer's research demonstrates that being intellectually challenged and having predictable taxation on our mental acuity can have the effect of a finger in the dike, holding back the degenerative processes leading to both Alzheimer's and dementia. This research also concluded that as we hit our 50s and beyond, there is an exigency on ensuring that we have riddles to ponder, problems to solve, and things to fix. The brain is a muscle that atrophies without use. One gentleman told me that after six months of retirement, he could sense the dulling in his cerebral muscle, along with signs of slowed thinking and sluggish articulation.

According to various studies and the American Gerontological Association, exercise and physical activity is directly related to successful aging. Three hours of exercise a week can increase your lifespan by five years.[5] In fact, physical *inactivity* is a predictor of things to come: increased falls, fractures, heart disease, respiratory disease, diabetes, and more! It's not a pretty picture. A more specific point to consider is that muscle mass declines by 1–2% a year past the age of 50 (if we're not addressing the matter) and this affects our strength, our endurance, and our balance. That fact alone should be enough to get all of us pumping some iron on a weekly basis. Not only will you feel better, this type of exercise has been shown to improve cognitive ability as well—so you'll not only know when someone is insulting you, you'll be able to flex your bicep to stop them.

Much of what we think of as aging is really just a by-product of inactivity and poor nutrition, and it's not hard to change that.
—Miriam Nelson, physiologist, USDA Research Center on Aging

The Gerontological Society of America reported on a study that showed fitness training resulted in significant increases in brain volume for people aged 60–79.[6] A cyclical relationship exists between body, mind, and spirit. It is difficult at times to explain, but, once experienced, it is well understood. One research study has shown that people who engaged in physical activity at least twice a week had a lower risk of dementia than those who were less active. In addition, starting to exercise more after midlife was shown to lower the risk of dementia.[7] Another discovery of significance is the corporeal-cognitive spark—the fact that physically challenging exercise actually "sparks" mental acuity. So, challenging the mind helps the body and challenging the body helps the mind.

Vitamin C3: Curiosity

On a flight home from Australia, I sat next to a PhD physicist from the University of Washington. At that time he was in his late 70s, still teaching and researching. I asked him why he wasn't retired, as was expected of a man his age. His answer was, "There's so much yet to learn," and he enthusiastically began describing his latest upper atmospheric physics research project. When I saw the sparkle in Dr. Clark's eyes as he spoke, I realized how good it would be if more seniors had their heads in the clouds of higher learning. Curiosity guarantees a pulse in the brain and a reason to keep our bodies healthy. The role of mental alertness cannot be overestimated, and neither can the benefits of a desire to grow. Once a person reaches a point where he no longer wants to learn or grow, it is time to order the tombstone. It need not be formal education that we pursue; it can be self-taught or experiential learning. The important thing is to have the curiosity and desire to grow. Age is an uphill road. Learning and tasks that demand mental alertness keep us in gear. Those of us who stay neutral in this area will quickly find we are going backward. Rigorous mental function helps to both facilitate productivity in later years and strengthen our need and desire to be active.

I personally believe that curiosity is the fountain of youth. I've met those who are 40 years old who are lacking in curiosity and seem prematurely old. And I've met others who are 80 years old who are possessing curiosity and show up as eternally young.

Vitamin C4: Creativity

I've long been enthralled by elderly artists in their 80s and 90s who seem as keen and perspicacious as people half their age. I once listened to an interview with a Canadian artist in her 90s, whose lucidity of thought and spry articulation was inspiring. She also confirmed my suspicions about the virtues of creative engagement in our later years. She talked about the aforementioned curiosity being razor-sharp as well. She reasoned that artists have developed a *discipline of observation* that requires seeing what others, who are less curious, might miss. A creative soul looks at the shoreline and sees something new every day. This might help explain why we have so many septuagenarian and octogenarian musicians still on tour. It might also explain why Peter Drucker was able to write a business bestseller in his 90s, and Warren Buffett is still active. Of course, you don't have to be renowned to be creative and to keep the powers of observation working. You just have to be curious, intrigued, expressive, and intentional.

A couple of other gems: The same elderly artist mentioned that her secrets were a profoundly diminished sense of self-consciousness; regularly scheduled, intellectually stimulating luncheons with people younger than herself; and two ounces of Canadian rye whiskey each evening for good measure!

Vitamin C5: Charity

Studies continue to surface around the ameliorative effects of charitable living on quality and longevity of life. Those who think about helping others often talk about how such charitable preoccupations lessen the degenerative effects of stress associated with worrying. Even if we didn't live a day longer because of charitable pursuits, we no doubt would live better.

Research from the Corporation for National and Community Service indicates that those who give of themselves boost their self-esteem and also gain a sense of more control over their own life: "In particular, older volunteers report lower mortality rates, lower rates of depression, fewer physical limitations, and higher levels of well-being. Older Americans who volunteer frequently live longer and report less disability."[8] There is an observable difference in the aging of the soul between the self-absorbed person and the selfless one. Giving to others, volunteering, and being a part of meaningful, significant activities seem to help promote healthier attitudes, which in turn improve one's health and contentment in life.

Once lethargy infects a person's body, it seems to quickly invade the mind and spirit as well. Soon energy levels are lower, the mind becomes less perspicacious, and optimism is affected as well. We cannot wait to feel energy to become fit; we need to foster a discipline of fitness in order to gain energy. The action precedes the feeling. Positive physical regimens like weightlifting, dietary discipline, and regular physical checkups add years to our lifespan. Just as important, these regimens add quality to the years we live. Why live to be 90 only to drag through 30 of those years with low energy and waning enthusiasm? Let's use our minds, engage our bodies, and nurture our spirits.

Aging reflects the relationship of time on our being. Aging describes, in large part, the state of our bodies. *Old,* however, describes our state of mind. It has always been a matter of great interest to me to discover the spiritual and attitudinal aquifer that supplies the fountain of youth.

There is no denying the effects of time on our bodies. Although we can slow certain physical impacts, we cannot prevent them altogether. Hair turns gray or falls out. Skin wrinkles. Senses like hearing and sight can begin to dull—as can short-term memory function. As George Burns once quipped: "You know you're getting older when everything hurts, and what doesn't hurt doesn't work."

Though our outward man perishes, our inward man is renewed day by day.
—The Apostle Paul's letter to Corinth

Equally immutable as the decaying dynamic of physical being is the constantly renewing and refreshing dynamic of our inner being. This dynamic of engaged living until the day we die is not automatic but is accomplished by the purposeful and intentional discipline of those souls who choose to *live* every day. They accept the inevitability of death but have chosen not to give death a head-start in their souls. Attitude becomes a matter of preeminence, for attitude is the rudder that steers the ship on this journey. Release the rudder for a single day and you can sense a sort of existential seasickness. Release it for a week, and you will drift aimlessly or be tossed on the rocks. Release the rudder for any longer period and shipwreck is inevitable. This is a truth I have witnessed time and again on the retirement landscape.

Challenge Your Body, Mind, and Spirit

Going forward, it will be more beneficial to choose a posture of proactive health rather than get caught up in the health-care system. You need to decide that this will be a vigorous and involved stage of life as opposed to a withdrawing and "retiring" stage. You can make the preparations you feel are necessary (such as long-term care insurance), but the greatest impact to your health will be rendered by the New Retirementality decisions you make for holistic well-being, such as:

- *Work out your heart on a regular basis by walking, jogging, or some other aerobic exercise.* As stated above, three hours of exercise per week adds five years to your life expectancy. It decreases depression, diabetes, and cancer rates—and helps you sleep better. Cardiovascular challenge replenishes oxygen into your cellular system and improves the function of both body and mind.

- *Engage in regular, light weightlifting.* Lifting holistically produces not just physical strength and resilience but attitudinal and internal strength as well.
- *Maintain physical intimacy.* The head actuarial at a leading insurance company told me of a conversation he had with a 75-year-old woman who was rated for a 20-year life insurance policy by his company. Having never seen this happen before, he called the woman to ask for the secret to her great health. Her reply: "Frequent and frantic sex."
- *Schedule charitable and altruistic activity into every week.* Those who feel a sense of purpose live longer and better.
- *Don't join the "moan and groan" sorority or fraternity.* Of course, we will all have joints that hurt or don't work as well as they did, but we don't have to linger on them. Pessimism leads to an expedited health decline.
- *Engage in work or activities that utilize your talents and challenge your brain.* Years ago, I read a quote from a Dr. Russell Clark, a 103-year-old real estate developer: "Continuing to work keeps the mind sharp and the body healthy, which aids in maintaining a positive attitude." This is as true today as it was when I first read it.
- *Drink a little coffee to start your engine and a little red wine to wind it down.* You've seen the studies. Cheers!
- *Examine your soul each day with reading, prayer, and self-check of motives in word and actions.* Forgive those who offend and love those who don't deserve it. It has been said that "grace is getting what we don't deserve, and mercy is not getting what we do deserve."

Stay focused on healthy living and follow some of the great examples of active and vibrant 80- and 90-year-olds. Your health habits will have a major impact on both your quality of life and the quantity of income available for that life. Think of health habits as an investment—in yourself. Physical discipline leaks over into mental focus, and mental focus and perspicacity leak over into introspection and a meaningful examination of your life. It is the body influencing the mind, which is influencing the spirit, and the cycle continues back through the mind now inspired and the body now energized.

In the old Greek myth of Narcissus, a man who becomes enamored with his own reflection in a pool eventually dies of starvation, because he cannot stand to leave his own image. We use the term *narcissism* to describe individuals who are consumed with themselves. In the study of successful aging, a lesson seems to appear later in life, this time as a wrinkled Narcissus beholding his image in the same pool of water. But instead of being enamored with himself, he becomes self-pitying at the sight of his decline and appearance. He wallows in so much self-pity that he will not leave to do anything to reverse his decline.

Americans generally feel that retirees have too little influence in the country today. This will change as new retirees keep their connections alive, remain relevant, redefine the life stage, and work toward impacting their communities, workplaces, and societies.

The New Retirementality has no time for a self-pitying stare into one's aging image. We must follow the ageless image within us—and stay connected to this world.

CHAPTER

Don't Go It Alone

The best interest of the patient is the only interest that matters.
—Dr. William Mayo

I have spent the better part of my life living in Rochester, Minnesota, home of the world-renowned Mayo Clinic, an organization that has a well-earned reputation for excellence in health care. All of my children, at some point, have had surgeries there, and one observation my wife and I have made is how transparently sensitive and caring the practitioners have been. In a realm that is often populated by practitioners who can come off as detached and overly scientific in their approach, it is always a breath of fresh air to encounter a professional who truly seems to have your best interests at heart.

At the Mayo Clinic this is no accident of personality or culture. It is by design. Early in the development of the clinic, the Mayo brothers stated that the culture would be built upon three core principles: competence, caring, and integrity. Everyone in the organization, from the top of administration to those mopping the halls, is inculcated with these cultural principles of operation. I hope they can continue this culture in an age where quantity (seeing more patients) is more important than quality (spending more time with patients).

I cite the Mayo example as an analogy to what we should expect to receive when we are seeking financial advice. After our health, our concern for our financial well-being occupies a high place on our totems of life. *Wealth care* ought to be approached with the same level of competence, caring, and integrity that has proven to produce great results in the realm of health care.

The temptation to put our own interests ahead of those whom we ought to be serving can, and does, manifest in every realm, whether it be a doctor recommending a procedure, a mechanic recommending a repair, or a financial advisor recommending a fund. In every realm of practice we will find the good, the bad, and the ugly. Many people have been financially harmed by incompetence, by a lack of concern and negligence, or by a lack of integrity in their financial matters, just like they may have been harmed by the same inadequacies in their health-care pursuits or other matters of life.

If you have a bad experience with a doctor, do you neglect medical care? Think of your money management as fiscal health. For every selfishly motivated financial salesperson, there is a highly competent and personable professional out there who has built his reputation helping others reach their goals by putting clients' interests first. We simply need to know how to distinguish one from the other. It can be easy to be fooled. In this chapter we will discuss finding someone who is competent, caring, and trustworthy for the very simple reason that saving yourself the stress is worth the price of oversight in the long run.

Some of the reasons I think it is worth considering hiring a competent professional include:

1. We don't always know what we don't know.
2. We are tempted to follow the crowd.
3. Individual investors historically underperform the indexes because they react emotionally to market events.
4. It is time consuming and stressful to manage money on a day-to-day or week-to-week basis.

We Don't Always Know What We Don't Know

Remember the online brokerage ads and the do-it-yourself proponents who wanted you to believe that nobody is to be trusted and that you should do this all on your own? Call me stupid, but when I'm looking to blame someone for making the wrong financial moves, I find myself at the top of the list. I have made more than my share of mistakes—many of which would have been avoided with professional consultation. The opposite also holds true. There have been instances when my instincts were right and I allowed a professional to talk me out of a decision. But on the whole, I would rather find someone worthy of my trust and not have all the stress myself. In my case, I work with someone who advises *and* consults with me when I think I have an idea. The bottom line is that we need someone worthy of our trust.

We Are Tempted to Follow the Crowd

Bubbles happen in the markets because everyone is doing the same thing; it also happens to be the worst possible thing we could be doing at the time. The common thread through bubbles is greed, whether that greed is institutional or individual. The dot-com bubble happened because everyone thought the Nasdaq run would never end, while tech start-ups were burning cash like it was so much refuse. The reality check came with a thud. The housing bubble happened because people were cajoled into thinking their homes could only go up in value—and that, too, ended with an economy-shocking and recession-inducing thud.

Where are the masses rushing to next? Bonds? Risky income-producing investments? Cryptocurrencies? Take your guess. One thing you can be sure of is that human nature will not change: people will follow other people, and the majority will get burned. It's good to seek some contrarian advice now and then. We are emotionally driven creatures, and the behavioral finance demonstrates that these emotions fool us and lead into poor financial decisions most of the time.

As with most things in life, you get what you pay for. That I can buy a stock for only $7 doesn't mean I'm going to profit from that purchase. In fact, because it is so easy and inexpensive to buy in and out of that stock, the odds are increased that I will act on impulse and trade in and out at the wrong times. *More important than the cost of making an investment is the quality of that investment.*

You can easily go broke in a short time at \$7 a trade. As Warren Buffett said, "With enough insider information and a million dollars, you can go broke in a year."

Individual Investors Historically Underperform the Indexes because They React Emotionally to Market Events

Dalbar has been reporting on individual investor trends for 25 years—their findings almost always indicate that while individual investors may beat the markets in the short run, they almost always underperform them in the long run. In fact, Dalbar reported that in 2018, the average investor was a net withdrawer of funds, "but poor timing caused a loss of 9.42% on the year compared to an S&P 500 index that retreated only 4.38%."[1] While a loss is always bad, in this case individual investors lost 100% compared to the S&P! Having a trusted professional who can help you achieve your goals is well worth the expense.

The self-directed, do-it-yourself approaches were motivated with good intentions, but most of us have neither the expertise nor the needed attention span to successfully manage such a proposition. Morningstar reports that individuals who use a trusted financial advisor will, on average, see almost 2% more in returns than those who go it alone. A study that was issued by Vanguard reported that clients who used a financial advisor saw returns of approximately 3% more than those who managed their funds on their own.[2]

The point is to have as much money as possible available for you to do with what you want. We can be our own worst enemy when it comes to reaching this point. Know your ability, availability, and attention span, do what is best for you in the long run, and make sure you get help where you need it.

It Is Time-Consuming and Stressful to Manage Money on a Day-to-Day or Week-to-Week Basis

I see many folks who are what I would call "hobbyists" with their money—they devote a great deal of time to market news, stock and fund prices, and the latest breathless headlines on CNBC. However,

I rarely see such a hobbyist who is not fairly high strung and experiencing manic periods of financial stress. I have often joked with the do-it-myself crowd that their first investment should be in Procter & Gamble, the maker of Pepto-Bismol, because their consumption will surely be going up. There will always be stress around financial decision making, but you need to choose between the stress of finding the right advice or the stress of advising yourself on a day-to-day basis.

Some people manage their own stock and/or mutual fund portfolios and get acceptable returns. Some of these do-it-yourselfers are truly savvy investors, and others are fortunate beneficiaries of a bull market (or they simply are missing bear markets) and good timing. I have a friend named Darryl who retired from IBM as an engineer in his mid-fifties. He and another engineer friend named Charlie created a long-term investment strategy after studying every retirement income model they could get their hands on and interviewing a number of planners. They went all out in creating their strategy after concluding "We think we can do this." Darryl doesn't do anything casually. He commits 100% to everything he puts his hands on. He and Charlie spent countless hours studying and re-studying, just like you'd expect engineers to do. They borrowed a baseline algorithm from a well-known retirement income scholar and went to work building their plan for investing and income. Knowing you are capable is one thing; actually wanting to carry the weight of responsibility is quite another.

As fate would have it, they retired at the worst possible time (late 2008) and the markets tanked, but Darryl and Charlie stuck to their plan because they were convinced it was the proper way to manage their money.

And guess what? Their plan worked. So, I have no doubt some people can navigate these choppy and scary waters on their own, but you'd better be as diligent and as smart as Darryl and Charlie were. I asked him to send their plan to me—here's the note he sent, along with the plan:

> *Here is a somewhat simplified version of the spreadsheet recreated back when I was first planning to retire. Previous versions had separate return assumptions for fixed vs. equities and*

simple/automatic portfolio rebalancing. We created a "statistical model" capability where we could randomize inflation and portfolio rates of return and run sort of a "Monte Carlo"–like simulation, but this version doesn't have all that stuff. I think it's all pretty self-explanatory.

I read it over. If you're not the engineering type, you would likely find it daunting. There are lots of moving parts, assumptions, and rebalancing maneuvers that need to be attended to. I came to the personal conclusion that, even though I understood it, I didn't want to be saddled with the distractions and anxieties of managing such a plan on my own.

Holding Your Ground

Another phenomenon I have witnessed with retirees and their money is that the more your portfolio grows, the more you may feel the need to get some help in making the right financial decisions. Many people seem quite content to remain alone while *growing* their assets, but that mindset is subject to change when the issue shifts to *protecting* those assets. Once you reach this stage of life you know with visceral certainty that you don't have another lifetime to gather what you will now rely on for sustenance.

Ask yourself these two questions:

1. Do I know everything I need to know about asset allocation, asset protection, tax-reduction strategies, risk management, and estate management?
2. Do I want to invest the time and effort to learn these issues? Do I want to continue to invest the time it takes to keep up with the markets and remain competent as an investment manager?

If you answered "yes" to these questions and have the time and interest in devoting yourself to building and protecting your assets, then you can go it alone. One caveat: don't assume you can possibly know all there is to know. Even if you want to do it on your own, it would be wise to pay for a consultation and get some direction from a professional money manager who knows her way around the brambles of managing risk, tax consequences, and more. Some professionals consult for an hourly or one-time fee.

If you know exactly what you want to own (stocks, bonds, mutual funds, etc.), know how to go about buying those holdings at the best price, and are not bothered by the stress of keeping up, then you may be a candidate to do it on your own. This assumes that you are well informed and can keep up on those holdings for any changes that could threaten the security of your investments.

Finding a Wealth-Building Partner

Because of the nature of my work, I have met literally thousands of brokers, advisors, planners, bankers, and accountants. All of these professionals are clamoring for your business. Some of these professionals I would trust my financial life to because of their integrity and competence. Others I wouldn't give a wooden nickel to because of their self-centeredness and lack of competence. Some of them are so busy selling that they don't really keep up with the products they are supposed to be expert in. They just keep telling the same story and selling the same products to everyone. Others I have met listen with great curiosity to each of their clients to figure out a strategy that is best for their clients, and then work hard to earn their clients' trust and loyalty.

Maybe you have heard or read stories or have had a bad experience yourself with a self-serving broker or advisor. "Once burned, their fault; twice burned, my fault," you tell yourself. There are some bad (read selfish) and good apples out there. You need to establish a clear profile of the type of person you want to work with and start interviewing until you find a match that feels right to you. Finding a match is as much about personal chemistry as it is financial philosophy.

After observing this wide range of integrity/competence, I have developed the following criteria for interviewing a financial professional. Use this assessment after talking to a professional, and you will greatly increase your odds of finding the wealth-building partner you need.

1. *What was your first impression of the individual?* Was she personable and respectful, or officious, self-absorbed, overly saccharine-coated, or arrogant? The individual's personality is a good indicator of the kind of service and attention you can expect to receive down the road should problems or concerns arise.

2. *What kind of questions did the financial professional ask you?* Did he ask more about your money and the size of your portfolio, or more about your life scenarios, financial experiences, and goals?

3. *Did the financial professional demonstrate good listening skills?* Did she carefully summarize your concerns, goals, and level of risk tolerance? If you get the feeling you are not dealing with a good listener, move on. If the individual is paying close attention now, you know that is what you can expect later. If the individual pretends to listen but just charges ahead with an agenda that seems to miss the point of what you told her, move on. If the professional dominates the conversation, get out as fast as you can!

4. *Did the financial professional explain matters in a language you could understand, or did he use jargon and talk over your head?* Those who talk over your head probably want to keep you in the dark or simply aren't smart enough to make matters understandable. Anyone who makes you feel stupid is not worthy of your business. A sure sign of competence is the ability to make complex matters seem simple and understandable. A good advisor will also be a good teacher and will help you improve your financial well-being. A good advisor isn't afraid of having a smart client!

5. *Is the financial professional willing to disclose her own personal holdings?* You would be amazed at the number of financial professionals whose personal financial lives are in disarray. There are also many who are not buying what they are selling. If financial professionals are trying to sell something they don't own, I want to know why. If you find an advisor who does for her clients what she does for herself, you have a greater potential for trust.

6. *Does the financial professional have a track record that can be documented?* Unless you want to be somebody's guinea pig, you should ask to see the professional's performance record. Check to see that the individual has done well in down

markets as well as in up markets. Ask for references and talk to those who have been clients for a long period. You can conduct a background check on an advisor at finra.org (www.finra.org/Investors/ToolsCalculators/BrokerCheck/).

7. *Does the financial professional articulate a clear philosophy regarding investments and wealth building?* If the professional doesn't have a clear philosophical compass that has been fine-tuned through experience, he is more likely to be one of those individuals who follows the crowd or the firm's latest recommendation. The dime-a-dozen advisor who sells whatever he is told to sell is not the person you are looking for. I like to see advisors who are comfortable talking about their mistakes as well as their victories—a good investment philosophy borrows from the lessons of both failure and success.

8. *Ask the financial professional how and why he got into this business.* In his response you will hear answers ranging from seemingly being on a mission to help other people to seemingly only pretending to be on a mission to help other people but really on a mission to help himself. I read between the lines on this answer. I want to get the sense that the financial professional is fascinated about money matters, curious about people, and motivated by his work.

If you walk out of an interview satisfied that these bases have been covered, you have a greater chance of partnering with a trustworthy individual. Cunning individuals may have the ability to fake these integral characteristics, but they cannot fake them for long. You want a concerned and competent professional who is in the profession for the right reasons. You want to find out what the person's motives are. After taking him or her through the preceding questions, you will have a fairly good indication.

A Personal Safety Net

When I was building an addition onto my home for our new baby boy, I decided I wanted to do some of the work myself to save money. I had a little experience doing electrical wiring and decided to tackle it with a little consultation. The builder agreed to inspect my work before the official inspector came in. When I was done with the wiring, the builder came to check my work. When he came to the last connection I had made, he showed me how I had erred and informed me that it could have easily started a fire. Then and there I decided some projects are far too important to try to tackle alone with a limited degree of experience. I believe that retirement or emancipation planning is one of those projects.

Even with the wealth of free online information available, when I travel to a faraway place, I like to get the advice of a trusted travel agent who has actually been there. I have found that faraway places don't always look and feel as pleasant as they appear in the brochure. Sure, I pay more by not doing it on my own, but my travel agent provides me with two intangibles that I value: experience and confidence. I want the peace of mind that comes from knowing I will not have unpleasant surprises when I arrive. I think of a good financial professional as a tour guide in a fiscal maze.

Guides of every description can be found today: "advisors" who are paid up-front and back-end commissions for the investment they're recommending, advisors who charge a one-time fee to design an investment plan; advisors who charge consultation fees by the hour, to advisors who charge a percentage of assets under management. The first is to be avoided. The other three deserve to be vetted. You can find a person and an arrangement you will be comfortable with in today's financial marketplace. Good financial professionals are worth their weight in gold.

You have a greater chance of reaching your emancipation goals with guidance, accountability, and coaching. A good advisor will provide you with all of these. It simply comes down to finding someone you can trust—someone who wants the satisfaction of helping you reach your goals, not using your funds to reach theirs.

Notes

Chapter 1

1. Laura Davidow Hirschbein, "William Osler and *The Fixed Period*: Conflicting Medical and Popular Ideas about Old Age," *Archives of Internal Medicine* 161 (September 24, 2001), https://deepblue.lib.umich.edu/bitstream/handle/2027.42/83267/LDH%20Osler.pdf;sequence=1.
2. Dora L. Costa, "The Evolution of Retirement: An American Economic History, 1880–1990," National Bureau of Economic Research Series on Long-Term Factors in Economic Development (University of Chicago Press, 1998).
3. Social Security Administration, "Life Expectancy for Social Security," https://www.ssa.gov/history/lifeexpect.html.
4. Mark Mather, Linda A. Jacobsen, Kelvin M. Pollard, "Aging in the United States," The Population Reference Bureau Report (Population Reference Bureau, 2015), https://www.prb.org/wp-content/uploads/2016/01/aging-us-population-bulletin-1.pdf.

Chapter 2

1. "1 In 3 Americans Have Less Than $5,000 In Retirement Savings, New Research Finds Waning Confidence in Social Security, Americans Expect to Work Longer," Northwestern Mutual (2018), https://news.northwesternmutual.com/2018-05-08-1-In-3-Americans-Have-Less-Than-5-000-In-Retirement-Savings.
2. Sudipto Banerjee, "Trends in Retirement Satisfaction in the United States: Fewer Having a Great Time," Employee Benefits Research Institute (2016), https://www.willistowerswatson.com/en/press/2018/02/globally-employees-are-feeling-financial-stress.
3. "2017/2018 Global Benefits Attitude Survey," Willis Towers Watson (2017), https://www.willistowerswatson.com/en/press/2018/02/globally-employees-are-feeling-financial-stress.

Chapter 3

1. Robert Delamontagne, *The Retiring Mind: How to Make the Psychological Transition to Retirement* (Fairview Imprints, LLC, 2011).

2. Nicole Maiestas, "Economy Needs 'Unretired,'" *Orange County Register* (December 12, 2012), https://www.rand.org/blog/2012/12/economy-needs-unretired.html.
3. Robert Powell, "Practice Retirement before Leaping into Leisure," *MarketWatch* (May 11, 2012), https://www.marketwatch.com/story/practice-retirement-before-leaping-into-leisure-2012-05-11.
4. E.M. Horner, *Journal of Happiness Studies* 15 (2014): 125, https://doi.org/10.1007/s10902-012-9399-2.
5. Jamie Chamberlin, "Retiring Minds Want to Know," American Psychological Association (January 2014), https://www.apa.org/monitor/2014/01/retiring-minds.
6. Chunliang Feng, Li Wang, Ting Li, and Pengfei Xu, "Connectome-based Individualized Prediction of Loneliness," *Social Cognitive and Affective Neuroscience* 14, no. 4 (April 2019): 353–365, https://doi.org/10.1093/scan/nsz020.
7. Robert Powell, "What Makes People Truly Happy in Retirement?" TheStreet (April 22, 2019), https://www.thestreet.com/retirement/what-makes-people-truly-happy-in-retirement-14931975.
8. United States Government Accountability Office, "Report to the Special Committee on Aging, U.S. Senate," Older Workers: Phased Retirement Programs, Although Uncommon, Provide Flexibility for Workers and Employers (June 2017), https://www.gao.gov/assets/690/685324.pdf.
9. Ibid.

Chapter 4

1. "How Many American Workers Participate in Workplace Retirement Plans?" Pension Rights Center (January 18, 2018), www.pensionrights.org/publications/statistic/how-many-american-workers-participate-workplace-retirement-plans.
2. "The State Pension Funding Gap: 2016," PEW (April 12, 2018), https://www.pewtrusts.org/en/research-and-analysis/issue-briefs/2018/04/the-state-pension-funding-gap-2016.
3. Pension Benefit Guaranty Corporation, "Annual Report 2018," https://www.pbgc.gov/sites/default/files/pbgc-annual-report-2018.pdf.
4. Richard Eisenberg, "The Next Retirement Crisis: America's Public Pensions," *Forbes* (October 22, 2018), https://www.forbes.com/sites/nextavenue/2018/10/22/the-next-retirement-crisis-americas-public-pensions/#441b620926f2.
5. John Mauldin, "The Pension Storm Is Coming to Europe—It May Be the End of Europe As We Know It," *Forbes* (October 3, 2017).
6. Barbara Griffina, Beryl Hesketh, and Vanessa Lohaa, "The Influence of Subjective Life Expectancy on Retirement Transition and Planning: A Longitudinal Study," *Journal of Vocational Behavior* 81, no. 2 (October 2012): 129–137, http://dx.doi.org/10.1016/j.jvb.2012.05.005.

7. Peter Finch, "The Myth of Steady Retirement Spending, and Why Reality May Cost Less," *New York Times* (November 29, 2018), https://www.nytimes.com/2018/11/29/business/retirement/retirement-spending-calculators.html.

8. Hanna van Solinge and Kène Henkens, "Living Longer, Working Longer? The Impact of Subjective Life Expectancy on Retirement Intentions and Behaviour," *European Journal of Public Health* 20, no. 1 (October 12, 2009): 47–51, http://eurpub.oxfordjournals.org/content/20/1/47.abstract?sid=1510875d-0fc7-42f5-9482-e32c28790c2e.

9. M. E. von Bonsdorff, K. S. Shultz, E. Leskinen, and J. Tansky, "The Choice between Retirement and Bridge Employment: A Continuity Theory and Life Course Perspective," *International Journal of Aging and Human Development* 69 (2009): 79–100.

10. B. Hesketh, B. Griffin, and V. Loh, "A Future-Oriented Retirement Transition Adjustment Framework," *Journal of Vocational Behavior* 12 (2009).

11. "Aegon Retirement Readiness Survey 2018: A New Social Contract" (June 6, 2018), https://www.aegon.com/research/reports/annual/aegon-retirement-readiness-survey-2018-a-new-social-contract/.

12. Viktor Frankl, *The Doctor and the Soul* (Vintage, 1986).

Chapter 5

1. Renee Stepler, "Led by Baby Boomers, Divorce Rates Climb for America's 50+ Population," Pew Research Organization (March 9, 2017), www.pewresearch.org/fact-tank/2017/03/09/led-by-baby-boomers-divorce-rates-climb-for-americas-50-population/.

2. B. Ashforth, *Role Transitions in Organizational Life: An Identity-Based Perspective* (Routledge, 2000).

3. M. Wang and K.S. Schultz, "Employee Retirement: A Review and Recommendations for Future Investigation," *Journal of Management* 36 (2010): 172–206.

4. K. Henkens, H. van Solinge, and W.T. Gallo, "Effects of Retirement Voluntariness on Changes in Smoking, Drinking and Physical Activity among Dutch Older Workers," *European Journal of Public Health* 18 (2008): 644–649.

5. Rob Walker, "When Early Retirement Turns into a Bore," *New York Times* (February 16, 2018), https://www.nytimes.com/2018/02/16/business/early-retirement-a-total-bore.html.

Chapter 6

1. Linda P. Fried, "Making Aging Positive," *The Atlantic*, June 1, 2014, https://www.theatlantic.com/health/archive/2014/06/valuing-the-elderly-improving-public-health/371245/.

2. Ibid.

3. Dan Starishevsky, "5 Ways to Start the 'Purpose' Conversation with Clients," *Investment News,* November 19, 2018, https://www.investmentnews.com/article/20181119/BLOG09/181119918/5-ways-to-start-the-purpose-conversation-with-clients.
4. Viktor Frankl, *The Doctor and the Soul* (Penguin Random House, 1986).
5. John Wallis Rowe and Robert L. Kahn, *Successful Aging* (Dell, 1999).
6. Jennifer M. Ortman, Victoria A. Velkoff, and Howard Hogan, "An Aging Nation: The Older Population in the United States." Report Number P25-1140, May 2014, https://www.census.gov/content/dam/Census/library/publications/2014/demo/p25-1140.pdf.

Chapter 7

1. "NEFE Sponsors Think Tank on Retirement Income Decumulation," *Nefe Digest* (January/February 2008), https://www.nefe.org/_images/nefe-digest/pre-2014/January-February-2008.pdf.

Chapter 8

1. Peter Hudomiet, Andrew M. Parker, and Susann Rohwedder, "Many Americans Follow Nontraditional Paths to Retirement: Cognitive Ability and Personality Traits Influence This Process," Rand Corporation, 2018, https://www.rand.org/pubs/research_briefs/RB10022.html.
2. "Globally, Employees Are Feeling Financial Stress," Willis Towers Watson, February 21, 2018, https://www.willistowerswatson.com/en/press/2018/02/globally-employees-are-feeling-financial-stress.
3. Art Swift, "Most U.S. Employed Adults Plan to Work Past Retirement Age," Gallup, May 8, 2017, https://news.gallup.com/poll/210044/employed-adults-plan-work-past-retirement-age.aspx?g_source=link_NEWSV9&g_medium=TOPIC&g_campaign=item_&g_content=Most%2520U.S.%2520Employed%2520Adults%2520Plan%2520to%2520Work%2520Past%2520Retirement%2520Age.
4. Andreas Kuhn, Jean-Philippe Wuellrich, and Josef Zweimüller, "Fatal Attraction? Access to Early Retirement and Mortality," *Vox,* March 25, 2012, https://voxeu.org/article/fatal-attraction-access-early-retirement-and-mortality.
5. Steve Vernon, "Does Working Longer Increase Your Lifespan?" CBSNews.com, March 8, 2010, https://www.cbsnews.com/news/does-working-longer-increase-your-lifespan/.
6. University of Michigan, "HRS: Health and Retirement Study," http://hrsonline.isr.umich.edu/sitedocs/databook/inc/pdf/HRS-Aging-in-the-21St-Century.pdf.
7. Jamie Chamberlin, "Retiring Minds Want to Know: What's the Key to a Smooth Retirement? Tend to Your Psychological Portfolio as Much as Your Financial One, Researchers Say," American Psychological Association, *Monitor* 45, no. 1 (January 2014), https://www.apa.org/monitor/2014/01/retiring-minds.

8. Ibid.
9. Transamerica Center for Retirement Studies, "13th Annual Retirement Study," 2012, www.transamericacenter.org/resources/tc_center_research.html.
10. Transamerica Center for Retirement Studies, "18th Annual Transamerica Survey," https://www.transamericacenter.org/retirement-research/18th-annual-retirement-survey/full-survey-results-compendium-report.
11. Ibid.

Chapter 9

1. Leisa D. Sargent, Mary Dean Lee, Bill Martin, and Jelena Zikic, "Reinventing Retirement: New Pathways, New Arrangements, New Meanings," *Human Relations* 66, no. 1 (2013): 3–21, https://journals.sagepub.com/doi/10.1177/0018726712465658.
2. Debra Auerbach, "Generational Differences in the Workplace," Career Builder, August 27, 2014, https://www.careerbuilder.com/advice/generational-differences-in-the-workplace.
3. Wan He, Daniel Goodkind, and Paul Kowal, "An Aging World: 2015," U.S. Census Report Number P95-16-1, March 28, 2016, https://www.census.gov/library/publications/2016/demo/P95-16-1.html.
4. Tammy Binford, "Changing Times Highlight Need for Employers to Adapt to an Aging Workforce," *Diversity Insight*, August 16, 2018, https://hrdailyadvisor.blr.com/2018/08/16/changing-times-highlight-need-employers-adapt-aging-workforce/.
5. "SHRM Foundation's Effective Practice Guidelines Series: The Aging Workforce: Leveraging the Talents of Mature Employees," SHRM Foundation, 2014, https://www.shrm.org/hr-today/trends-and-forecasting/special-reports-and-expert-views/Documents/Aging-Workforce-Talents-Mature-Employees.pdf.
6. David Bloom and David Canning, "How Companies Must Adapt for an Aging Workforce," *Harvard Business Review*, December 3, 2012, https://hbr.org/2012/12/how-companies-must-adapt-for-a.
7. Kenneth Terrell, "Age Discrimination Common in Workplace, Survey Says," AARP, August 2, 2018, https://www.aarp.org/work/working-at-50-plus/info-2018/age-discrimination-common-at-work.html.
8. University of Wisconsin Oshkosh, Division of Online and Continuing Education, "Learning in Retirement," https://uwosh.edu/oce/personal-and-professional-development-programs/learning-in-retirement/.
9. AARP Foundation, Experience Corps, https://www.aarp.org/experience-corps/.
10. Transamerica Center for Retirement Studies, "18th Annual Transamerica Retirement Survey," Transamerica Institute, 2018, https://www.transamericacenter.org/docs/default-source/retirement-survey-of-workers/tcrs2018_sr_18th_annual_worker_compendium.pdf.

11. Richard W. Johnson, Janette Kawachi, and Eric K. Lewis, "Older Workers on the Move: Recareering in Later Life," AARP, 2009, https://assets.aarp.org/rgcenter/econ/2009_08_recareering.pdf.

12. American Institute for Economic Research, "New Career for Older Workers," AIER, 2015, https://www.aier.org/sites/default/files/Files/Documents/Webform/AIER_OWS.pdf.

13. Guidant Financial, "2019 Small Business Trends: A Look at the State of Small Business in 2019," https://www.guidantfinancial.com/small-business-trends/.

14. Melanie Curtin, "Attention, Millennials: The Average Entrepreneur Is This Old When They Launch Their First Startup," *Inc.*, May 17, 2018, https://www.inc.com/melanie-curtin/attention-millennials-average-entrepreneur-is-this-old-when-they-found-their-first-startup.html.

15. Kerry Hannon, "Proof That Entrepreneurs Are Older Ones," *Forbes*, August 5, 2018, https://www.forbes.com/sites/nextavenue/2018/08/05/proof-that-the-most-successful-entrepreneurs-are-older-ones/#25f7042642dd.

16. Andrea Coombes, "10 Tips for Boomers to Become Entrepreneurs," *MarketWatch*, January 14, 2013, https://www.marketwatch.com/story/10-tips-for-boomers-to-become-entrepreneurs-2013-01-14s.

17. Ibid.

Chapter 10

1. "Research Shows Old Age Is Getting Younger All the Time," *The Conversation*, April 16, 2015, https://theconversation.com/research-shows-old-age-is-getting-younger-all-the-time-38556.

2. William J. Chopik, Ryan H. Bremner, David J. Johnson, and Hannah L. Giasson, "Age Differences in Age Perceptions and Development Transitions," *Frontiers of Psychology*, February 1, 2018, https://www.frontiersin.org/articles/10.3389/fpsyg.2018.00067/full.

3. Ibid.

4. Ibid.

5. Becca R. Levy, Martin D. Slade, Robert H. Pietrzak, and Luigi Ferrucci, "Positive Age Beliefs Protect against Dementia Even among Elders with High-risk Gene," *PLOS|One*, February 7, 2013, https://www.ncbi.nlm.nih.gov/pubmed/29414991.

6. Ibid.

7. David Weiss and Frieder R. Lang, "'They' Are Old but 'I' Feel Younger: Age-group Dissociation as a Self-protective Strategy in Old Age," *Psychology and Aging* 27, no. 1 (March 2012): 153–163, https://psycnet.apa.org/doiLanding?doi=10.1037%2Fa0024887.

8. Marlene Cimons, "Clichés about Only Being as Old as You Feel Are Starting to Have Scientific Backing," *The Washington Post*, April 14, 2018, https://www.washingtonpost.com/national/health-science/cliches-about-only-being-as-old-as-you-feel-are-starting-to-have-scientific-backing/2018/04/13/4ccd9c4a-3125-11e8-8abc-22a366b72f2d_story.html?utm_term=.5fe5370ad79b.

9. Howard Gleckman, "A New Snapshot of Older Adults in the U.S.," *Forbes*, May 4, 2018, https://www.forbes.com/sites/howardgleckman/2018/05/04/a-new-snapshot-of-older-adults-in-the-us/#4461632739d7.

10. United States Department of Labor, Bureau of Labor Statistics, "Civilian Labor Force Participation Rate by Age, Sex, Race, and Ethnicity," https://www.bls.gov/emp/tables/civilian-labor-force-participation-rate.htm.

11. Mike Waters, "Jim Boeheim Set to Be Oldest Coach in D-1 History: 'Go as Long as You Can Do a Good Job,'" Syracuse.com, November 7, 2017, https://www.syracuse.com/orangebasketball/2017/11/syracuse_basketball_coach_jim_boeheim_will_keep_on_coaching.html.

12. Ibid.

13. Ibid.

14. Kevin J. Gries, Ulrika Raue, Ryan K. Perkins, Kaleen M. Lavin, Brittany S. Overstreet, Leonardo J. D'Acquisto, Bruce Graham, W. Holmes Finch, Leonard A. Kiminsky, Todd A. Trappe, and Scott Trappe, "Cardiovascular and Skeletal Muscle Health with Lifelong Exercise," *Journal of Applied Physiology* 125, no. 5 (November 2018): 1636–1645, https://www.physiology.org/doi/abs/10.1152/japplphysiol.00174.2018?journalCode=jappl.

15. Ian Johnston, "Septuagenarians Go to the Gym More Than Any Other Age Group, Claims Nuffield Health," *Independent*, April 24, 2015, https://www.independent.co.uk/life-style/health-and-families/health-news/septuagenarians-go-to-the-gym-more-than-any-other-age-group-claims-nuffield-health-10200249.html.

16. American Geriatrics Society, https://www.americangeriatrics.org/programs/reframing-aging.

17. Jessica Nordell, "Is This How Discrimination Ends?" *The Atlantic*, May 7, 2017, https://www.theatlantic.com/science/archive/2017/05/unconscious-bias-training/525405/.

Chapter 11

1. Leisa D. Sargent, Mary Dean Lee, Bill Martin, and Jelena Zikie, "Reinventing Retirement: New Pathways, New Arrangements, New Meanings," *Human Relations* 66, no. 1 (2013): 13, https://journals.sagepub.com/doi/10.1177/0018726712465658.

2. Lewis Wallace, "Trending for 2016: The Senior-Friendly Gym," Antioch College, WYSO, December 30, 2015, https://www.wyso.org/post/trending-2016-senior-friendly-gym.

Chapter 12

1. "Cents and Sensibility: Schwab Survey Finds that Americans Define Wealth in Very Different Ways," Charles Schwab, June 21, 2017, https://pressroom.aboutschwab.com/press-release/schwab-investor-services-news/cents-and-sensibility-schwab-survey-finds-americans-defi.

2. "2018 Insights on Wealth and Worth," Bank of America, 2019, https://www .ustrust.com/articles/insights-on-wealth-and-worth-2018.

Chapter 13

1. Generations Ahead Study, Allianz Life Insurance Company of North America, September 25, 2017, https://www.allianzlife.com/about/news-and-events/ news-releases/Generations-Ahead-Study-2017.
2. "If You Couldn't Work, Could You Maintain Your Lifestyle?" Disability Resource Insurance Center, http://di-resource-center.com/disability-insurance-statistics/.

Chapter 15

1. Dr. Michael F. Rooizen, MD, *The RealAge Makeover: Take Years Off Your Looks and Add Them to Your Life* (HarperCollins, 2005).
2. John Wallis Rowe and Robert L. Kahn, *Successful Aging* (Dell, 1999).
3. Alan D. Castel, *Better with Age: The Psychology of Successful Aging* (Oxford University Press, 2018).
4. Susan Pinker, "The Secret to Living Longer May Be Your Social Life," TED 2017, https://www.ted.com/talks/susan_pinker_the_secret_to_living_longer_ may_be_your_social_life/transcript#t-547678.
5. Stanley J. Colcombe, Kirk I. Erickson, Paige E. Scalf, and Jenny S. Kim, "Aerobic Exercise Training Increases Brain Volume in Aging Humans," *The Journals of Gerontology Series A Biological Sciences and Medical Sciences* 61, no. 11 (December 2006): 1166–1170, https://www.researchgate.net/publication/6633161_ Aerobic_Exercise_Training_Increases_Brain_Volume_in_Aging_Humans.
6. Ibid.
7. Christopher Bergland, "Physical Activity Improves Cognitive Function: Regular Physical Activity Can Improve Brain Function throughout a Lifespan," *Psychology Today*, April 9, 2014, https://www.psychologytoday.com/us/blog/ the-athletes-way/201404/physical-activity-improves-cognitive-function.
8. "The Health Benefits of Volunteering for Older Americans: A Review of Recent Research," Corporation for National & Community Service, May 2012, https://www.nationalservice.gov/pdf/healthbenefits_factsheet.pdf.

Chapter 16

1. "Quantitative Analysis of Investor Behavior Study," DALBAR, Inc., March 25, 2019, https://www.dalbar.com/Portals/dalbar/Cache/News/PressReleases/ QAIBPressRelease_2019.pdf.
2. Mark P. Cussen, "How Financial Advice Can Boost Your Returns," Investopedia, September 28, 2018, https://www.investopedia.com/articles/personal- finance/102616/how-much-can-advisor-help-your-returns-how-about-3-worth.asp.

About the Author

Mitch Anthony is the founder and president of mitchanthony.com, an organization dedicated to helping companies around the world communicate openly and honestly with their clients and customers.

For two decades, Mitch has shown individuals how to move from a financial plan focused strictly on the numbers (return on assets) to one focused on Return on Life™ (ROL)—living the life you want with the money you have. He personally consults with many of the largest and most recognized names in the financial services industry on ROL planning and relationship development.

Mitch is the cofounder of ROLAdvisor, a coaching community that is helping financial planners better serve their clients through Life-Centered Planning™, a process that puts ROL front and center in the financial planning process.

Mitch has been named one of the financial services industry's top "Movers & Shakers" for his pioneering work. He has partnered with numerous universities in the United States and Canada to develop life-centered financial planning programs for their undergraduate programs. Mitch is a popular speaker and contributor to both local and national media and host of the inspirational radio feature *The Daily Dose*, heard on approximately 100 radio stations nationwide.

A prolific author, Mitch has written more than 10 books. *The Financial Lit-Kit* (Insights Press), a series of three beautifully illustrated books, teaches children about the importance of financial responsibility. *Defining Conversations: A Little Book About a Big Idea* (Insights Press) explores the importance of having meaningful conversations in a world increasingly focused on texting.

Mitch and his wife, Debbie, live in Rochester, Minnesota, where they are involved in many philanthropic endeavors at both the local and international level. Living examples of the new retirementality, neither Mitch nor Debbie has plans to ever retire.

For more information about Mitch and his organization, visit www.mitchanthony.com, or contact him at Mitch@mitchanthony.com.

Index

401(k) plans, 33
  distributions, delay, 40
  tapping, 97–98
403(b) plans, 33

A
Abilities
  optimization, 126
  usage, fulfillment factor,
    76
About Schmidt (movie), 116
Acceptance (grief,
    stages), 20
Achievement, 123
Activities, connecting
    (Retirementality
    Profile), 116–117
actual age, old age
    (contrast), 38
Advocacy, 30–31
Aerobic exercise, usage, 166
After the honeymoon (LEAN
    stage three), 26
Age
  age-related actuarial
    probabilities, 37
  attitude, 103–107
  defining, avoidance, 58
  feeling, 102

Ageism
  images, replacement/
    embracing, 108
  impact, 93–94
  perspectives, change, 108
  public health campaign,
    impact, 103
  stereotypes
    dispensing, 107–108
    replacement, 108
Ageless wonders,
    examples, 11
Aging
  culture-based
    views, 103–107
  mastery, 158–160
  negative views, 102
  pitfall, 159
  quality, 159
  retirement
    characteris-
    tic, 72, 77–78
  stereotypes,
    patience (absence), 85
  success
    attitudes, 161
    indicators, 159–160
  transition, 157
  Vitamin Cs, usage, 160–166

Aging Well (Vaillant), 84
Aimlessness, feeling, 27
Albert, Marv, 107
Alcohol, drinking
    (increase), 27
Alcott, Amos, 9, 158
Altruism, 123
Altruistic activity,
    scheduling, 167
American Institute for
    Economic Research,
    retirement study, 96
Anger (grief, stages), 20
Anxiety, 82
Apostle Paul, letter to
    Corinth, 166
Arayama, Takao, 104
Asset
    allocation/protection,
        knowledge, 174–175
    ownership, 175
Atchley, Robert C., 2
Attitude, impact, 56
"Attitude instrument",
    attention, 58
Attitudes, endurance, 63–65
Attitudinal factors, 156
Autonomy, motivation,
    14–16

B
Baby Boomers
    decisions, 98
    influx, 65
    withdrawal
        perspective, 111

"bag-lady/poor-old-man
    syndrome", 135
Balance, 123
    defining, 126–127
    finding, 75
    retirement
        characteris-
        tic, 71, 74–75
    social balance,
        importance, 28
Balance sheet, 28
Bargaining (grief, stages), 20
Bass, Richard, 104
Bates, Kathy, 116
Better with Age (Castel), 159
Bills, paying, 140–141
Bismarck, Otto von, 3–5
Bloom, David, 93
Body
    activity, 78
    challenge, 58, 166–168
Boeheim, Jim, 104–105
Bolles, Richard, 19
Boredom
    approach, 13–14
    avoidance, 43
    ease, 115
    identification, problem, 50
    impact, avoidance, 51
    predictor, 44
Bored-O-Meter,
    usage, 150–151
Bosses, youth, 91–93
"Bouncing around",
    willingness, 91
Bridge employment, 39–40

*Bridging the Generation
    Gap* (Gravett/
    Throckmorton), 92
Bronte, Lydia, 9
Brown, Hubie, 107
Bucket List (movie), 152
Bucket lists/listers, 43, 152–153
Buck, Jack, 106
Buffett, Warren, 121,
    125, 128, 164
Burns, George, 64, 166

C
Canning, David, 93
"Captain Coupon"
    syndrome, 25
Careers
  change
    example, 57–58
    success, 96
  changers, happiness, 96
  extension, advice, 90–91
  success, 129
Carey, Harry, 106
Caring, 169
Carroll, Lewis, 71
Castel, Alan D., 159
Challenge (Vitamin C2),
    160, 162–163
Challenge, loss, 44
Chaney, John, 105
Chapman, Elwood, 67
Charitable activity,
    scheduling, 167
Charity (Vitamin C5),
    160, 165–166

Chopik, William, 102
Churchill, Winston, 64, 157
Clark, Russell, 167
Closed community,
    avoidance, 46–47
Coaching, 104–105
Coffee, drinking, 167
Cognitive decline,
    retirement delay
    (impact), 84
Communicativeness,
    decrease, 27
Competence, 169
  absence, 175
  range, 175
Competition, need, 115
Confidence, increase, 159
Connections, Retirementality
    Profile, 116–117
Connectivity (Vitamin C1),
    82, 160, 162
Coombes, Andrea, 97
Couple's conundrum,
    preempting, 25
Creative potential,
    increase, 10
Creativity (Vitamin
    C4), 160, 164
Culture, principles, 169
Curiosity (Vitamin C3),
    160, 163–164
Current life portfolio, 75

D
Dalbar, investor trends, 172
Da Vinci, Leonardo, 79

Defined benefit
    (DB) plan, 33
    defined contribution (DC)
    plan, contrast, 34
    funding, 35
Defined contribution
    (DC) plans, 33
Delamontagne,
    Robert, 20, 45
Dementia
    development, 116–117
    risk, decrease, 84, 163
Denial (grief, stages), 20
Dennis, Helen, 97
Depression, 82
    feelings, experience, 27
    grief stage, 20
Desired life portfolio, 75
Devine, Patricia, 108
Diminishing returns, law
    (impact), 46, 48–49
"Dinosaur Floor", 89
Disability,
    avoidance, 159–160
Disease
    avoidance, 159–160
    ease, relationship, 48
Disposition, position
    (relationship), 40–41
Dissatisfaction, sense, 137
Divorce rates, increase, 49
Do-it-yourself
    approaches, 172
Douglass, Frederick, 136
Dream income, 139–140
Drucker, Peter, 64, 164

Dufouil, Carole, 84
Dylan, Bob, 101

E
Efforts
    direction, 40
    quality,
        improvement, 127–128
Elderly, term (objection),
    65
Eliot, George, 72
Embarking (LEAN stage
    two), 24–26
Employees, positive
    transition, 31
Employment
    bridge, 39
    chains, 16
Emptiness, formula, 46, 47
Encore (AARP), 87
    winners, 59–60
Encouragement,
    importance, 106–107
"Enduring",
    characteristic, 64
Energy level, 115
Engagement,
    meaningfulness, 86–87
Engagements,
    selection, 149–150
Ens, Marie, 58–59
Entrepreneurship, 96
    assistance, 97
    elasticity, 98
    franchise,
        consideration, 98

investment requirement,
    assessment, 97–98
preparation, 97
shared
    workspaces, usage, 98
Entrepreneurs,
    maturity, 96–99
Entrepreneur's
    Source, The, 908
Erikson, Erik/Joan, 54
Estate management,
    knowledge, 174–175
Esteem
    loss, 26
    redefining, 137
European debt cri-
    sis, institutional
    obligations
    (impact), 36
Existential preparation,
    importance, 70
Expectations, forecast, 145
Experience
    growth, work (impact), 76
    investment, 68
    ranking, 153–154
    richness, increase, 9
    usage, 40
Exploration, 123
    agenda, 61–62
    mode, 86
Extraction dates, 11–13

F
Faith, Nathan, 22
Family, 123

closeness, importance, 147
    importance, 95–96
Fascination,
    replacement, 45–46
Fear, impact, 53–54
Female parolees (Encore
    winners), 60
Financial advisors, resource
    (ranking), 145–146
Financial challenges, 36
Financial creativity, usage, 15
Financial issues, 152
Financial life planning, 135
Financial motivators (bridge
    employment), 39–40
Financial needs,
    hierarchy, 136–140
    pyramid, 137f
Financial planning, 69–70
    importance, 144
Financial professionals
    business entry,
        reasons, 177
    hiring, reasons, 171–174
    investment/wealth
        building philosophy,
        clarity, 177
    language,
        understandability/
        usage, 176
    listening skills, 176
    personal holdings,
        disclosure
        (willingness), 176
    track record, 176–177

Financial services industry,
    public education
    improvement, 70
Finke, Michael, 28
Fiscal well-being, 148
Fitness training, impact,
    163
Forced retirement, 28–29
Formal Phased Retirement
    Programs, 29
Formal phased retirements,
    employer-based
    programs, 30
"Fountain of age", 54
Franchise, consideration,
    98
Frankl, Viktor, 40–41, 61,
    63, 79, 128
Freedman, Mark, 87
Freedom, 123
    attention/rebalancing, 68
    income, 139
    investment, 68
    redefining, 137
Freeman, Morgan, 152
Freud, Sigmund, 136
Friedan, Betty, 54
Fried, Linda, 53
Friends, closeness
    (importance), 147
Frisch, Michael B., 118
Frustration, impact, 45–46
Fulfillment, 123
    defining, 126
Full-time jobs, retention, 81

G

Generations Ahead Study, 135
Generations at Work (Zemke/
    Raines/Filipczak), 91
Gift income, 139
Gifting, 136
Goals
    articulation/achievement,
        partnering, 131
    pursuit, freedom, 128
    reaching, satisfaction,
        129–130
Go-go time frame, 37
Golden-ager, term
    (euphemism), 93
Golden parachutes, 19
Graebner, William, 7
Grandparents, average
    longevity
    (determination), 38
Great Depression, 4
Great recession, impact, 8
Greed, impact, 171
Green, Theodore, 11
Grief, stages, 20–21

H

"Habits of mind", 107
Happiness, 123, 130
    defining, 124–126
Haynes, Marion, 67
Health
    attention, 95
    improvement, 159
Heart, workout, 166

Hierarchy of Needs
(Maslow), 134–136
History of Retirement
(Graebner), 7
Hitler, Adolf (rise), 4
Hobbies, 144
cost, 137
engagement, 48, 114–115
interest, 20
satisfaction (decrease), 26
Hobbyists, 172–173
Holmes, Oliver
Wendell, 1, 53
Holzmann, Jac, 92
Horner, Elizabeth Mokyr, 26
Houdini, Harry, 121
Humor, sense (importance),
64
Hypothetical retrospect,
impact, 62–63

I
Ideal week, retirement
example, 25, 114f
Identity
loss, 44, 49–50
sense, 81
sense, 10
"I have to" crowd, 55–56
Imbalance, lines (crossing),
110
"I'm done" crowd, 55
"I'm inspired"
crowd, 55, 56–58
Impact, creating/making, 115

Improvisational challenges,
assumption, 39–41
Income
addition, need, 115
dream income, 139–140
freedom income, 139
gift income, 139
safety income, 138–139
survival income, 138
"Income for Life", 134–135
Income/outcome
worksheet, 140, 141f
Individual investors, index
underperformance,
170, 172
Individual retirement
accounts (IRAs),
usage, 34
Individual retirement
attitude (IRA), 36
importance, 45
Industrial Age, work
(perspective), 79
Industrialization, advent, 2
Informal phase retirement
arrangements, 30
INSERM, 84
Insights
attention/rebalancing,
68
investment, 68–69
Intangibles, types, 124–130
Integrity, 169
range, 175
Intrigue, loss, 44

Investment
  arenas, 68
  crowd, following
    (avoidance),
    170, 171–172
  financial professional
    philosophy, clarity, 176
  freedom, 68
  knowledge, 174–175
  money, investment, 67
  rebalancing, 68–69
  self-investment, 67
Isolation, 44

J
Job discrimination, 93–94
Joel, Billy, 59
Jogging, regularity, 166
Johnson, Richard W., 96
Jones, E. Stanley, 123

K
Kahans, Eva, 26
Kauffman FastTrac, 97
Kawachi, Janette, 96
Kenagy, H.G., 7
Knowledge
  awareness, 170–171
  investment, 68
  transfer, 30–31

L
Labor force participation,
  increase, 29
Law of diminishing returns,
  impact, 46, 48–49

LEAN. *See* Looking ahead,
  Embarking, After
  the honeymoon,
  Negotiating balances
Learning-in-retirement
  space, local
  offerings, 94
Lear, Norman, 108
Leisure
  activities, interest, 85
  attainment, 47, 48–49
  benefits, 81
  cost, 152
Lethargy, impact, 165
Levy, Becca, 103
Lewis, Eric K., 96
Life/living
  attention, areas, 68
  attitude, impact, 56
  balance, 74, 109
    lines, 110
  closed community,
    avoidance, 46–47
  continuation, outlook, 40
  current life portfolio, 75
  desire, payment, 134
  emptiness, 46, 47
  engagement,
    continuation, 159–160
  examination/
    direction, 71–78
  expectancy, 5
    age-related actuarial
      probabilities, 37
    increase, 104
  expectations,
    realism, 46–49

experiences, usage, 59–60
exploration
   agenda, 61–62
   mode, 86
imbalance, lines, 110
improvisational stage,
   retirement
   (comparison), 40
insecurity, 128
meaningfulness,
   decision, 131
mental/attitudinal
   approach, 38
monotone living, 44–45
passive approach,
   problems, 64–65
purposefulness,
   benefits, 544
pursuit, resources
   (usage), 131
quality, increase, 108
quarantine, problem, 47
rebalancing, 68
responsibilities, 86
retirement profile, 72–78
satisfaction, "sugar rush", 26
self-rating, guide, 118
stagnation, formula, 47–48
Lifespan,
   lengthening, 36, 37–39
Lifestyle. *See* Retirement
   rewards, 21–22
Listlessness, formula, 47
Living rich, 121–122
Location, staying/
   going, 146–147

Loneliness, 44
Longevity, 83–84, 162
   age attitude,
      impact, 103–107
Longevity Factor, The
   (Bronte), 9
Looking ahead (LEAN stage
   one), 21–24
Looking ahead, Embarking,
   After the honeymoon,
   Negotiating balances
   (LEAN), 19
   stages, 21–28
Low-income homeowners
   (Encore winner), 60

M
Making Aging Positive
   (Fried), 53
Mandatory retirement,
   usage, 3
Man's Search for Meaning
   (Frankl), 63, 79
Market events, emotional
   reaction, 170, 172
Markey, Michele, 97
Marriage, strain/tension, 115
   increase, 27
Maslow, Abraham, 133–140
Mastery, sense, 64, 158–160
Matsko, Briggs, 134–135
Mayo, William, 169
Means/meaning, gap
   (bridging), 121
Me-centric lifestyles,
   problems, 48–49

Mellencamp, John, 80
Mental alertness, role
  (impact), 164
Mental function,
  maintenance, 159–160
Mental health, work-
  ing retirement
  (necessity), 83
Mental stimulation, change/
  reduction, 821
Mental well-being, 148
Middle age, expansion,
  80–81
Midlife crisis, 58–63
Mille, Agnes de, 124
Mind
  activity, 78
  challenge, 58, 166–168
Mindset, change, 15
Mission mode, 86
Miura, Yichiro, 104
"Moan and groan"
  sorority/fraternity,
  avoidance, 167
Money
  allocation, 154–156
  attention/rebalancing, 68
  importance, 91
  investment, 67
  management
    fiscal health,
      comparison, 170
    stress/time
      consumption, 172–174
  maturity, 10
  outliving, risk, 138–139

perspective, 134–136
saving, obsession, 25
spending, freedom, 134
stewardship, 130–131
Monotone living, 44–45
Montepare, Joann M., 84
Mortality rates, decrease, 165
Mortgage foreclosures, 1328
Motivation level, 115
Motives, self-check, 167
Mountain climbing, 104
Move, staying/going,
  146–148
Mussolini, Benito (rise), 4

N
Narcissism, 168
National Industrial
  Conference
  Board employees,
  retirement sales, 7
Negotiating balances (LEAN
  stage four), 27–28
Nelson, Miriam, 163
networks (creation),
  enthusiasm
  (decrease), 27
New Dealers, plans (testing),
  4–5
New IRA, 33
New Retirementality
  adoption, 135
  decisions, 166
  development, 72
  differences, 82
  perspective, 23

Nicholson, Jack, 116, 152
No-go time frame, 37
Nonfinancial challenges, 36
Nonfinancial retirement
    challenges, 81–82
Nuffield Health survey, 106

O
Observation, discipline, 164
O'Connor, Mary, 44
Old age, actual age
    (contrast), 38
Older people, health/
    cognitive status, 101
Older workers
    liability, 91
    work ethic, 91
*Older Workers on the
    Move* (Johnson/
    Kawachi/Lewis), 96
Older Workers Pension
    Act (1935), 5
Old, term
    objection, 65
Old, term (defining), 10–11
Online information,
    availability, 178
Osler, William, 3
Outdoors,
    enjoyment, 153–154

P
Paige, Satchel, 10–11, 64
Parents, average longevity
    (determination), 38
Part-time jobs, retention, 81

Part-time work, transition, 81
Pattern Makers League of
    North America, 4
Pauling, Linus, 64
Paycheck, absence
    (impact), 82
PBGC. *See* Pension Benefit
    Guaranty Corporation
Peale, Norman Vincent, 64
Pension
    benefit erosion,
        continuation, 36
    checks, Social Security
        payments (com-
        bination), 7
    establishment (1934), 4–5
    fund assets/liabilities, 36
    obligations,
        meeting (problem), 34
    plans
        promotion, 4
        usage, decrease, 35
    public pension obligations,
        scenario, 35–36
    shift, 19
    state pension
        plans, deficits, 34
Pension Benefit Guaranty
    Corporation (PBGC)
    obligations, examina-
        tion, 34–35
P.E.P. *See* Places, Experiences,
    and People
Personal missions, 86–87
Personal safety net, 177–178
Phased retirement, 28–29

Phelan, Jim, 105
Physical being, dynamic, 166
Physical function, mainte-
    nance, 159–160
Physical health, working
    retirement (necessity),
    83
Physical inactivity,
    impact, 162–163
Physical intimacy,
    maintenance, 167
Physical well-being, 148
Place of Rescue, 59
Places, Experiences, and
    People (P.E.P.), 61
    recording, 62
Planning, expectations
    (forecast), 145
Platinum parachutes, 19
Play
    downscaling, 151
    Retirementality
        Profile, 114–115
    work, balance, 151–153
Playcheck, collection, 76, 77
Poppler, Meredith, 118
Population Reference
    Bureau, age statistic, 6
Portfolio, growth, 174–175
Position, disposition
    (relationship), 40–41
"Position taken", 56
Possessions, worry, 125–126
"Practice retirement" idea,
    advocacy, 21–22
Prayer, usage, 167

Pre-Retirement
    Agreement, 49
Project Renewment
    (Dennis), 97
Psychological work issues,
    82
Public pension obligations,
    scenario, 35–36
Pursuit, meaningfulness,
    58–63

Q
Quality of Life Therapy
    (Frisch), 118

R
Rafferty, Bill, 107
Raines, Claire, 91
Rand Un-Retirement
    study, 20–21
Reading, usage, 167
Real Age (Roizen), 158
Reassurance, usage, 159
Red wine, drinking, 167
Re-firement, 111
Reflective exercise, 25
Reframing Aging
    Initiative, 107
Re-hirement, 111
Relational well-being, 148
Relationships, 111
    building, 15
    challenges, 81
    improvement, 126–127
Relaxation,
    attainment, 47, 48–49

Relevance
  loss, 89–90
  maintenance, 37
  need, 115
Renaissance, 111
  mode, 86
Renewal, quest
    (Retirementality
    Profile), 117–119
Resources
  attention/rebalancing, 68
  usage, examination, 131
Responsibilities,
    freedom, 153
Retirees
  disillusionment
    rates, 13–14
  satisfaction, Employee
    Benefits Research
    Institute study, 17
Retirement
  accounts, shift, 19
  age (prediction),
    Subjective Life
    Expectancy
    (usage), 37
  aging, 72, 77–78
  American Institute
    for Economic
    Research study, 96
  approach, 8
  artificial finish lines,
    removal, 9
  autonomy, motiva-
    tion, 14–16
  balance, 71, 74–75

  characteristics,
    identification, 71–78
  closed community,
    avoidance, 47–48
  coaches, increase, 80
  delay, impact, 84
  depiction, 20–21
  direction, 69–71
  divorce rates, increase, 49
  expectations,
    realism, 46–49
  exploration agenda,
    61–62
  failure, consumer
    responsibility, 70
  features/possibilities/
    parameters, financial
    service industry
    education, 70
  financial challenges, 81
  history, 1
  hype, 16–18
  ideal week, example, 114f
  illusions/delusions, 16–18
  length, planning, 69–71
  life profile, 71–78
  lifestyle
    boost, 6
    rehearsal, 21–22
  mandatory retirement,
    usage, 3
  Maslow, relationship,
    133, 137f
  mind-set, change, 53
  money, allocation, 154–156
  negative effects, 83–84

nonfinancial retirement
challenges, 81–82
numbers, increase, 7–8
picture, change, 70
planning
discussion, 70–71
success, 86–87
Pre-Retirement
Agreement, 49
priorities, 23
purpose
desire, 134
role, 148–149
purposefulness, 53
profile, 60–61
readiness
definition, 84–86
ranking, 145
Transamerica Center for
Retirement Studies
definition, 84–85
realities, 143–146
rearview mirror, 50–51
relaxation, attain-
ment, 47, 48–49
relic, 1–2
retirement-persona
profile, 25
sales, 7
satisfaction, factors, 28
savings, *Northwestern
Mutual
Planning &
Progress Study,* 17
scare tactics, 18
success, 79
consumer responsibility, 70

time/experimentation, 83
unnaturalness, 2, 13
vision, 71–73
voluntariness, impact, 50
work, 72, 76–77
choice, statistics, 81
working retirement,
importance, 83
worksheet, 25, 75
zone, adherence, 90–91
Retirementality
defining, 109
philosophical exam, 24
Retirementality Profile,
25, 112f–113f
connections, 116–117
play, 114–115
renewal, 117–119
work, 115–116
Retirementors, 44, 59
advice, 143
Retirementors Councils, 144
Retiremyths, 146–151
"Retire on purpose"
decision, 56–57
exercise, 60–61
Retiring Mind, The
(Delamontagne), 45
Re-tiring, perspective
(change), 110–119
Re-wirement, 111
Rich, redefining, 121
Risk management,
knowledge, 174–175
Robinson, Jackie, 10–11
Roizen, Michael F., 158

Role transitions theory, 50
Roosevelt, Eleanor, 136
Roosevelt, Franklin D., 4–6
RP-2000 Mortality Study, 83

S
Safety income, 138–139
S-aging, 78, 157
Sand, George, 143
Santana, Carlos, 10
Satisfaction
    defining, 127–128
    postdating, 14
Schweitzer, Albert, 64
SCORE, 97
Scully, Vin, 107
Second life, entry, 54–55
Security, 130
    defining, 128
Self-centeredness, 175
Self-coaching, 104–105
Self-confidence, increase, 10
Self-consciousness, sense, 164
Self-esteem
    increase, 165
    reduction, 103
Self-investment, 67
Self, redefining, 109
Self-reliance, factors, 159
Self-sufficiency,
    challenge, 159
Senior citizen, term
    (euphemism), 93
Seniority-based pay,
    performance
    (relationship), 93

Seniors (Encore winners), 60
Seniors, term (objection), 65
"Sense of mastery", 64, 158–160
Septuagenarians,
    analysis, 105
Sequence of Return Risk
    Y'All (S.O.R.R.Y.)
    factor, 155–156
Shakespeare, William, 48
Shared workspaces, usage, 98
Shaw, George Bernard, 56
Significance, 123
    defining, 128–129
Skinner, B.F., 136
SLE. *See* Subjective Life
    Expectancy
Sleep, lateness, 26
Slow-go time frame, 37
Social balance,
    importance, 28
Social challenges, 81
Socialness, decrease, 27
Social network,
    importance, 115
Social Security
    creation/problems, 5
    payments, pension checks
    (combination), 7
    resources, usage, 74
Social time, alone time
    (balance), 27–28
Society for Human Resource
    Management Mem-
    bers, Formal Phased
    Retirement Programs
    (percentages), 29

Sociology of Retirement, The
    (Atchley), 2
S.O.R.R.Y. factor. *See*
    Sequence of Return
    Risk Y'All factor
Soul
  desolation, 47
  self-examination, 167
Spirit
  activity, 78
  challenge, 58, 166–168
  depletion, 12–13
  desolation, 47
Spiritual pilgrimage, 117
Stagnation, formula, 47
State pension plans,
    deficits, 34
Stein, Michael, 72
Stein, Michael K., 37
Stereotypes. *See* Ageism
Strojny, Nancy, 97–98
Subjective Life Expectancy
    (SLE), 37–39
  retirement age
    predictor, 38
Success, 123
  defining, 129–130
  experience, 159
Super-septs, 101
Supervisor, order taking
    (willingness), 91
Support, presence, 159
Survival income, 138
Survival, relevance (impact),
    90
Sustainability, importance,
    91

T
Taft, William Howard, 4
Talents
  attention/rebalancing, 68
  investment, 68–69
  usage, fulfillment factor, 76
Tax-reduction strategies,
    knowledge, 174–175
Teaching, importance, 94–95
Technology
  impact, 91
  shifts, resistance, 92
Television, watching
    (increase), 26
Terkel, Studs, 64
Throckmorton, Robin, 92
Time
  addition, 82
  attention/rebalancing, 68
  maximization, 128–129
Transamerica Center for
    Retirement Studies,
    retirement readiness
    definition, 84–85
Transferable skills,
    importance, 96
Trappe, Scott, 105

U
Underemployment,
    advantages, 95–96
U.S. Government
    Accounting Office on
    Phased Retirements,
    research, 28–29
U.S. Senate, average age, 104
Utilitarian mode, 86

V

Vacation, 111, 151–153
    affordability, 152
    guilt, 152
    time, availability, 152
Vaillant, George, 84
Value
    examination, 79–80
    supply, 47
Vernon, Steve, 83
Vision
    creation, 72
    retirement
        characteristic, 71–73
Visioning
    exercise, 25
    process, 73
Vitale, Dick, 107
Vitamin Cs
    challenge (Vitamin C2),
        160, 162–163
    charity (Vitamin C5),
        160, 165–166
    connectivity (Vitamin C1),
        160, 162
    creativity (Vitamin C4),
        160, 164
    curiosity (Vitamin C3),
        160, 163–164
    usage, 160–166
VO_2 max, age-related
    reduction, 106
Vocation, 111
    importance, 148–149
Volunteer activities,
    impact, 148

Volunteering, 165
    activities, problems, 26
    importance, 148
    play, combination, 151
Volunteerism, 80

W

Wagner, Robert F., 4–5
Walking, regularity, 166
Wealth
    care, 170
    meaning, 122
    redefining, 121
Wealth building
    financial professional
        philosophy, clarity, 176
    partner, discovery, 175–177
Wealth-building partner
    impression, 176
Weather, importance, 147
Weekly activity, defining, 68
Weightlifting, usage, 167
Well-being
    responsibility, 40
    "sugar rush", 26
West, Scott, 111
What Color Is Your Parachute?
    (Bolles), 19
Wired, determination, 45
Wisdom
    investment, 68
    usage/application, 40
Work
    balance, factors, 115
    benefits, impact, 76
    continuation, 36–37

enjoyment, 115
enthusiasm level, 76
ethic, 91
  degradation, 2
expression, 76
fulfillment, factors, 76
impact, creating/
  making, 115
life, social aspects
  (absence), 151
modes, 86–87
motivation/drive, 115
negative impact, 12–13
people, interaction
  (quality), 76
play, balance, 151–153
quitting, 12
redefining, 80–83
Retirementality
  Profile, 115–116
retirement characteris-
  tic, 72, 76–77
social/intellectual benefits,
  requirement, 40
social network,
  importance, 115

work until age, optimum
  (determination), 38
Workers. *See* Older workers;
  Younger workers
future, planning, 31
retention, 30
Workforce
  exit/reentry, 81
  planning, 93
Working retirement,
  importance, 83
Workout regimen,
  importance, 105–106
Workplace
  age, reentry
    (determination), 51
  reemergence, 98

Y
Younger bosses, 91–93
Younger workers, impact,
  91

Z
Zweimuller, Josef, 83